God reveals Himself mightily through prayer as well as through trying times. Each page of this book abounds with surprise and delight as well as inspiring strategies for overcoming the everyday battles of life. *Fight Back With Joy* is a gift—one you can't afford to miss.

—Mark Batterson, lead pastor of
National Community Church in Washington, D.C.
and author of *New York Times* best-selling *The Circle Maker*

Margaret Feinberg is a strong voice of hope for us all. She is the real deal!

—Karen Kingsbury, #1 *New York Times*
best-selling author of *Angels Walking*

When you feel stuck in the rut of discouragement, there's no greater gift than rediscovering joy. With profound insight and poignant grace, Margaret Feinberg takes you on a journey toward joy that will reawaken your heart to the glee that comes with knowing God. You can't read this book and stay the same.

—Pete Wilson, senior pastor of
Cross Point Church in Nashville, TN
and author of *Plan B* and *Let Hope In*

Feinberg's story resonates deep within my heart. You'll be captivated by her skill in weaving together words, thoughts, and phrases—but even more beautiful is the way you'll be drawn closer to Jesus, our source of joy.

—Kay Warren, best-selling author and
cofounder of Saddleback Church in Lake Forest, CA

Through her signature beautiful storytelling, Margaret Feinberg gives us an inspiring story of the true power of joy. In these pages, you'll learn to defeat lifelong patterns of discouragement, discover strategies for overcoming everyday challenges, and have your heart awakened to the delight of being a child of God. In *Fight Back With Joy*, the world of the Bible and our world come together in a way that will transform your life forever. A must-read.

—Tim Clinton, EdD, president, American Association of Christian Counselors, executive director and professor of counseling and pastoral care at the Center for Counseling and Family Studies at Liberty University

Margaret Feinberg's courage, candor, and tender vulnerability are transforming. Her raw struggles touched deep places in my life and will in yours too. *Fight Back With Joy* will deepen your compassion, bring healing, and fortify your holy resolve to follow God through anything. This is a message the church needs to hear today.

—Jennie Allen, founder of If:Gathering and author of *Restless*

So good. Just so unbelievably good. I cried more tears than I have in a very long time while reading for so many reasons. Ridiculously moving, laced with the beauty, art, and the eternal tension of Scripture. Don't think of this book as a happy-clappy, naive approach to having life ripped away, but rather a difficult and conscious decision to encounter the darkness with light, to fight back deep sorrow with deep, lasting joy. No matter your personal fight, your life will be changed by reading this hope-filled book.

—Cherie Lowe, author of *Slaying The Debt Dragon*

FIGHT
BACK WITH
JOY

CELEBRATE MORE. REGRET LESS.
STARE DOWN YOUR GREATEST FEARS.

Margaret Feinberg

WORTHY®
PUBLISHING

Published by Worthy Books, an imprint of Worthy Publishing Group, a division of Worthy Media, Inc., 134 Franklin Road, Suite 200, Brentwood, TN 37027.

WORTHY is a trademark of Worthy Media, Inc.

HELPING PEOPLE EXPERIENCE THE HEART OF GOD

eBook available at www.worthypublishing.com.

Library of Congress Cataloging-in-Publication Data

Feinberg, Margaret, 1976– .
  Fight back with joy : celebrate more. regret less. stare down your greatest fears / Margaret Feinberg.
     pages   cm
  Includes bibliographical references and index.
  ISBN 978-1-61795-089-6 (tradepaper : alk. paper)
  1. Joy—Religious aspects—Christianity. 2. Suffering—Religious aspects—Christianity. 3. Breast—
Cancer—Patients—Religious life. I. Title.
  BV4647.J68F45 2014
  248.8'6196994—dc23

                                                                                    2014030902

Some names, identifying details, and medical information have been changed in this book to protect the privacy of the individuals involved.

This book is not intended to provide therapy, counseling, clinical advice or treatment or to take the place of clinical advice or treatment from your personal physician or professional medical health provider. Readers are advised to consult their own qualified healthcare physician regarding mental health or medical issues. Neither the publisher nor the author takes any responsibility for any possible consequences from any treatment, action, or application of information in this book to the reader. When a doctor's advice to a particular individual conflicts with the experiences and ideas presented in this book, that individual should always follow the doctor's advice.

Unless otherwise noted, Scripture is taken from the New American Standard Bible®, Copyright © 1960, 1962, 1963, 1968, 1971, 1972, 1973, 1975, 1977, 1995 by The Lockman Foundation. Used by permission. Scripture quotations marked MSG are taken from *The Message.* Copyright © 1993, 1994, 1995, 1996, 2000, 2001, 2002. Used by permission of NavPress Publishing Group. Scripture quotations marked NIV are taken from The Holy Bible, New International Version®, NIV® Copyright © 1973, 1978, 1984, 2011 by Biblica, Inc.® Used by permission. All rights reserved worldwide. Scripture quotations marked ESV are taken from the English Standard Version. © 2001 by Crossway Bibles, a division of Good News Publishers. All rights reserved. Scripture quotations marked NLT are taken from the Holy Bible, New Living Translation, copyright © 1996, 2004, 2007 by Tyndale House Foundation. Used by permission of Tyndale House Publishers, Inc., Carol Stream, IL 60188. All rights reserved. Scripture quotations marked NRSV are taken from the New Revised Standard Version Bible, copyright © 1989 the Division of Christian Education of the National Council of the Churches of Christ in the United States of America. Used by permission. All rights reserved. Scripture quotations marked NKJV are taken from the New King James Version®. Copyright © 1982 by Thomas Nelson, Inc. Used by permission. All rights reserved.

Italics added to direct Scripture quotations are the author's emphasis.

For foreign and subsidiary rights, contact rights@worthypublishing.com.

ISBN: 978-1-61795-089-6

Cover Design: Christopher Tobias, Tobias' Outerwear for Books
Interior Design and Typesetting: Christopher D. Hudson & Associates, Inc.

Printed in the United States of America

CONTENTS

Bonus Tracks

.000 | WHY WE LIVE JOYLESS LIVES

New Year's resolutions are so last year, according to my friends. Many of them instead choose to live by a single word, one that embodies what they most hope God would do in their lives during the coming year.

My friend Sarah selected *love* last year, which led her to mend ties with her estranged father. Then there was John, who chose *balance*. He hung a chart on his kitchen wall to track his days and make sure he spends enough time with his family. And after Patty picked *hope*, she enlisted friends to help her see the sunny side of every situation. When her pessimistic tendencies emerge, her friends give her a "hope nudge."

Seeing how this practice enriched my friends' lives, I dreamed about which word embodied the work I most wanted God to do in my life.

I had spent years listening for the sacred echoes, the repetitive voice of God in my life. I'd set out to scout for the divine, searching to better understand God through lesser-known biblical texts. And I had worked to shake myself from spiritual slumber and encounter the wonder of God all around.

During these God-journeys, a word kept bubbling inside me and fluttering about everywhere I turned. Only three letters and one tiny syllable: *joy*.

Could this be my word?

For most of my life, I had thought of joy as a natural byproduct of a life well lived. A complementary add-on, a tacked-on freebie. Like one of those late-night infomercials that promise, "But wait, there's more!" Maybe such a bonus was included: I never seemed to find it amid the packing materials.

With the holidays in my rearview mirror and a New Year just ahead, I determined it was time to pursue a joy-filled life. No need to wait for joy to arrive mysteriously in the mail one day. I needed to try spiritual practices that might nurture joy.

Only a few months in, I was less effective at living out my word than my friends had been. Some joy experiments were disasters—like creating a homemade worry-o-graph that raised my anxiety rather than lowering it, and trying to mandate kindness, which backfired and made me a crabbypants.

The silliest fiasco was the two weeks I committed to saying yes to everything. When I asked select friends and members of my online community to join me, I received a unanimous response: "That is wackytown!" Okay, only one person used that exact phrase, but everyone else hid behind excuses like "spread too thin," "too busy," and "no way I could do that."

Their responses surprised me, because I am *that* friend— the one always plotting the next caper. I'll call you at midnight to see if you want to try indoor skydiving, go on a ten-day juice fast, or score cheap airline tickets to Iceland. Sometimes I won't ask or tell you what we are going to do; I'll just send details on a treasure map of when and where to meet.

The chorus of "No!" should have alerted me that the Yes Experiment wasn't sustainable. Discouraged but not defeated, I decided to embark on the venture by myself.

I explained the details of the Yes Experiment to my husband, Leif.

"You're doing this? You're crazy, you know that?"

"Of course, but I'm *your* crazy."

"You're going to say yes to *every*thing?"

"Within reason. Don't worry, I won't sell our house for a dollar."

"Do *I* have to say yes to everything?" he asked.

"You can say no to anyone and anything you want," I explained. "But I'm agreeing to every request, including e-mails, texts, phone calls, tweets, and mail that's addressed to me."

"Does that mean when I ask you for something the answer is yes too?"

I nodded.

Leif stared at the floor, his mind sprinting through the implications. I wondered how long it would take him to figure out the possibilities for *bow chica wow wow.*

Within 2.8 seconds, a boyish grin slipped across his face.

Like a Florida kid caught in a Michigan snowball fight, I was ill-prepared for the assault of requests that came from all directions. Coworkers. Friends. Readers. Strangers. Solicitors. Salespeople. In the first few days, I made so many donations I had to start selling furniture and clothes on eBay to fund the Yes Experiment. I helped save animals and refugees and fund microloans. At least I think I did.

"Do you want to donate a dollar to Easter Seals?"

Yes.

"Would you read my fifty-thousand-word book on North American flora and see if you think it's any good?"

Yes.

"Would you like to leave a tip on the dollar granola bar you just purchased?"

Yes.

"Would you like to supersize your order?"

Yes.

Those types of asks were the most manageable. The great onslaught came from the office. My inbox exploded with requests for Skype calls, book endorsements, reprints, donations, mentoring, coaching, and more. While online, I said yes to every request to click, vote, or post. Within a half hour I knew I needed to stay far, far away from social media.

The Yes Experiment was causing me to do a lot without getting anything done. The unsustainable pace left me exhausted and empty, but my stubbornness prevailed.

I drove downtown to run errands on day four of the experiment. In a congested area of Denver, I noticed a man standing at the intersection, holding a clever cardboard sign that requested money for spaceship parts. As long as the light remained green, I could drive past and not have to buy a muffler for his intergalactic aircraft.

The light blinked yellow, and in a flash, an invisible force overtook my right foot. I stomped on the accelerator and sped through that red light with the gusto of Danica Patrick.

Why did I just do that?

Saying yes to everything was causing me to spend time and energy on the inconsequential, ignoring the people who mattered most. Rather than increase my joy, the Yes Experiment made me hypervigilant to avoid anyone who might ask for anything. This discipline was elbowing me away from the virtue of joy I sought.

My friends were right: this caper was flawed.

Joy is one of those words that has been overused, distorted into a cliché. Plastered on coffee mugs, necklaces, T-shirts, decorative pillows—even dish soap, this critical quality has been transformed into a trinket we rarely notice and almost never take seriously.

Many people live joyless lives because they don't understand what joy is, what joy does, how to discover joy, and what to do with it once they find it.

C. S. Lewis once described joy as "serious business," yet I assumed I could take joy lightly, capturing it in my free time like fireflies in a mason jar. I learned that you need much more than an experiment to unleash the power of joy. You need chutzpah, you need backbone, you need intentionality—and sometimes you need a crisis.

My crisis came in a flash flood of irony. I set out to conduct a joy experiment, but I became the test subject, the bubbling beaker of blue liquid, the living lab rat. Through a life-shattering diagnosis, I tumbled into uncertainty, anxiety, and pain. Along the way, I discovered what true joy looks like.

My crisis exposed the myths I believed about joy—such as the belief that fullness of joy is only available once we are in heaven and the illusion that joy is an emotion that exists apart from circumstances.

During the last year and a half, I felt my way through the darkness of despair and stared death in the face. Somewhere along the way God unveiled a spectrum of joy I had never experienced—from the joy expressed as lighthearted laughter in an impossible situation to the joy gained from hearing the deep voice of God during times of great pain. Through it all, I learned something startling:

**More than whimsy,
joy is a weapon we use to fight life's battles.**

Sure, the virtue of joy is an upbeat companion for life, but that is not the whole story. The true power of joy supersedes a chirpy disposition, candy-coated emotion, or saccharine fantasy. It's far more tangible than any magical notion of clicking your heels and discovering your bliss.

Joy serves a useful and mighty purpose. Sometimes it comes through others as a gift of grace, but just as often it requires intentionality.

God is an unconventional teacher. He uses paradox to imbue us with common sense, propels healing through pain, and hauls clarity into our lives through the most confusing circumstances. In my case, God interrupted my misguided joy experiment in order to take me on a joy expedition. This journey was fraught with depression and loneliness, tears and turmoil—using unlikely circumstances to deliver joy instead of destroy it.

But in order to realize that, I had to face the moment everyone fears.

.001 | A CHOICE THAT CHANGED EVERYTHING

As THE JULY SUN peeked over the horizon, I received the dreaded call.

My upper arm itched a few weeks earlier, and when I scratched the area, my thumb brushed against a knot. I paused, afraid to reach back and explore further. I willed myself to move. My fingers probed against my right breast, outlining the nickel-sized circumference.

Anxiety clutched my body. A second and third touch confirmed the solid intruder's presence.

Calm down, Margaret. It's probably nothing to worry about. Who gets breast cancer in her thirties?

I turned to my husband of almost a decade—my Leif, always a solid rock of strength in fearful moments—hoping he would say I was overreacting or hallucinating.

"Can you feel this?" I asked, pressing the tips of his fingers against my chest.

Concern shadowed his face. With his nod, I reached for a phone to schedule the mammogram.

Three days later, before a technician, I stood half-naked, skirted in a paper-thin hospital gown with icy bare feet. I initiated chitchat, but what do you discuss with someone tugging at part of your womanhood like it's pizza dough?

"Have you felt anything unusual?" she asked.

"Nothing like this," I said wryly. "I try to keep my lady parts out of pancake makers."

Without cracking a grin, the nurse clarified, "I mean any lumps or bumps."

The details of the discovery stuck in my throat. Maybe if I didn't say it aloud, the lump would disappear. Perhaps if I clung to denial long enough, the mass would vanish.

"Well, there's this, um, one small area," I confessed.

She jotted a note on her clipboard.

"I'm pretty sure it's nothing."

"Most lumps are just thick tissue," she explained. "But we have to be sure. Because you informed me, we're required to schedule an ultrasound."

"Is there a way to uninform you?" I asked.

"No."

A letter arrived in the mail two weeks later. The images returned clean: no signs of lumps, bumps, or thick tissue. I later discovered that 20 percent of mammograms miss finding dangerous masses, which is why speaking up is crucial.

Just as the technician predicted, the office insisted I return for an ultrasound. This time I found myself sprawled on a table with my arm raised high above my head like a schoolgirl begging the teacher to recognize her. Only I didn't want to be recognized. I wanted to disappear.

I eyed the screen but had no idea what I was seeing. The click of the digital camera froze a portrait of the lumpy villain I had found weeks before, but it also revealed a second hardened criminal. The radiologist excused herself, returning with the doctor. When I asked, "Is it cancer?" he avoided the question. I needed to schedule a biopsy.

Worst-case scenarios raced through my mind. I thought of a friend who died from cancer the previous summer, her body ravaged by treatment. Now I could see myself in her: the emaciated cheeks, the thin oxygen tube, the inability to lift a spoon to my cracked lips. I clenched my eyes tight, chasing away the mental images.

Time slowed to a leaden pace in the following days as I waited for the next appointment.

My third visit to the doctor's office played out like *Groundhog Day*. Again, I raised my hand in uncertainty. Again, I asked about cancer. Again, the doctor dodged the question.

The doctor located the first mass with precision, the image taunting me from the screen. He lined up a gauged needle and shot it through the center of the dark, uneven circle over and over. My chest became a pincushion.

When the doctor located the second mass, an unedited comment slipped from his lips: "This is the one I'm concerned about."

"What do you mean?" I asked.

Unaware he was thinking aloud, the doctor stiffened and backpedaled.

"More than ninety percent of our biopsies turn out to be benign," he said. "You have nothing to worry about."

I knew I did.

Toward the end of the procedure, he asked a nurse to let him see one of the syringes. I strained to catch a glimpse of the narrow tube. Out of the corner of my eye, I watched a somber expression sweep across his face.

That was the moment I knew.

I held out hope that perhaps I was wrong, that maybe I had misread the doctor's countenance. But deep inside, I knew.

The nurse said the weekend would slow results from the laboratory. She instructed me to call on Tuesday afternoon. But Tuesday never came.

Early Monday, the phone rang showing an unfamiliar number. I almost didn't answer. Leif and I were at Mount Hermon Conference Center outside of Santa Cruz, California, where more than forty of Leif's extended family members had gathered for the first family reunion in ten years. I was scheduled to teach morning sessions at the conference center that week, the first of which started in a matter of minutes.

As a rule, I avoid taking phone calls just prior to speaking, but the unknown number piqued my interest. I answered on a whim.

"This is Dr. Jones," the voice said. "Is now a good time?"

No. No, no, no.

As the physician spoke, my head dropped into liquid amber. Time halted. The conversation blurred.

Carcinoma.

Positive.

Both masses.

Surgery.

I'm sure he said more, but after *carcinoma* everything grew fuzzy. After the call, I stared at a wretched souvenir of the conversation: a scrap of paper on which I'd scrawled two recommended surgeons' names.

Dazed, I beelined to the field house, where Leif was busy preparing the PowerPoint slides.

"I have your microphone ready," Leif said.

He glanced up. I couldn't hide my apprehension.

"What's wrong?"

I took his hand, led him outside where we could be alone, and looked into his sky-blue eyes. I never spoke a word. Leif just knew. He always knows. My eyes are his second language.

He cloaked me in his arms and we stood motionless, knowing we had crossed a threshold through which we could never return. In the warmth of his strong embrace, I wondered where God was in all of this.

Did God ignite my heart's desire for joy in preparation for this moment? Is this why so many of the joy experiments didn't work out the way I hoped they would? Perhaps God was pumping the brakes, ever so gently, readying me for this moment, for the hard journey ahead.

"What if we fight back with joy?" I said to Leif.

"We're in this together no matter what," he replied, eyes swollen by tears.

With the morning session minutes away, I phoned my parents to inform them. My sweet, longtime Christian mother responded the way I suspect many moms whose guard is down would: with an expletive.

"Breast cancer doesn't run in our family," she protested.

The diagnosis busted a family myth—cancer happens to other people.

I delivered my talk that morning. Barely. Tears surged down my cheeks with the opening music, and holding myself together required my last ounce of strength. We corralled Leif's family to deliver the news at lunch. Everyone wanted to know what they could do to help.

"More than anything, I need each of you to be your funny, ornery selves," I said. "That's how to help us fight back with joy."

Throughout the rest of the week, Leif and his two bulky brothers exchanged love punches and razzed each other. We toured grand sequoias and took silly photos inside hollowed tree trunks. We threw a Mexican fiesta. Over the course of those precious days, we played Apples to Apples, grilled steaks, and ate way too much Alaskan smoked salmon.

Amid the revelry, the cancer loomed like Gollum in the shadows. Some days I had to dismiss myself to weep; others, I spent sequestered under the duvet, attempting to hide from the ominous news. Yet somehow my extended family offered what I needed most: a sense of normalcy, laughter, and joy.

When we arrived home in Colorado early Saturday evening, my parents stood in our living room, dinner already prepared. Their presence reminded me of the divine orchestration in the diagnosis. My parents live on a remote island in the Bahamas and only pass through Colorado twice a year. This was the Saturday they had long ago scheduled to visit.

On the heels of Leif's family gathering, including those who had flown in from as far as Alaska, Hawaii, and South Africa, I realized the remarkable timing. The date of diagnosis seemed perfectly, providentially timed so that I would be surrounded by family from around the world.

If I had heard someone else tell this story, I would have been skeptical. Watching these events unfold left me amazed. One week later and there would have been no cheery family reunion to soften the blow, no welcoming committee at my door. Even in the seriousness and tragedy of the moment, it was as if God was whispering: *I am with you. Yes, even in this.*

An image that haunts me from that first week was the sight of a family member slipping out of the room when I broke the news. I later learned that he went to weep on the deck. Though I never saw his tears, I glimpsed something in his eyes that I soon recognized in those who had encountered similar adversity: tenderness, gentleness, empathy.

Those who stared down the disease, along with their loved ones, were like brave warriors engaged in a mighty fight. Forged by fire and affliction, many bore scars from grappling with the dark enemy, somehow escaping if only with their lives.

They, too, had been ambushed. They knew the battlefield I approached all too well. Like them, I would ooze and burn and bleed. I was now a member of the guild no one wants to join. I discovered that once you're in, everyone lends a hand. Our shared experiences, desire to fight back, and will to survive bind us together.

These guilds don't only form around diseases. Soldiers who have served on the front lines exchange meaningful looks with other veterans. Bonds form among believers who endure a painful church split or a leader's moral failure. Solidarity emerges among parents whose children live with autism or ADHD. A powerful connection is felt among those who have lost a child.

Though the struggles we face are different, no one escapes this life unscathed.

Maybe your fight intensified during a traumatic injury or began with a foreclosure or bankruptcy. Perhaps you were handed divorce papers or you had to trod the painful road of a loved one's death.

Maybe you are battling the loneliness of an empty nest or the lingering disappointment that life didn't turn out as you hoped it would. Maybe you feel imprisoned by depression or trapped by a cantankerous boss or spouse. Maybe you are fighting with your parents or your kids.

Or maybe you're just fighting to stay sober.

All of us are in a fight. Others can fight *with* you, but no one can fight this *for* you.

You see the scars when you look in the mirror or into your soul. And you know you'll need to fight again tomorrow.

Everyone who wakes to confrontation and crisis—whether you picked the fight or the fight picked you—has an important choice: which weaponry will you choose? Cynicism and spite? Complaint and control? Or perhaps you are prone to deny and withdraw. To let your fleshy heart turn to stone. But there is another arsenal available to the daughters and sons of God.

From the day of the diagnosis, I felt compelled to choose a different type of weapon: joy. Such a selection might seem flippant and frivolous. One blunt friend called it "downright odd." If I had to cry ten thousand tears, I wanted joy to be the companion that carried me through. Joy would not deny the hardship, but would choose to acknowledge and face it no matter what the outcome.

I define *joy* as a spectrum of emotions, actions, and responses that includes gladness, cheer, happiness, merriment, delighting, dancing, shouting, exulting, rejoicing, laughing,

playing, brightening, blessing and being blessed, taking pleasure in and being well pleased.

The Bible insists that joy is more than a feeling; it's an
action. We don't just sense joy; we embody it by how we
respond to the circumstances before us.

What is the genesis of this joy? I believe that, at its
core, *joy emanates from the abiding sense of God's fierce love
for us.*

The tigerish love of God from which joy comes is foun-
dational to faith. God's love guards us, protects us, grows
us, strengthens us, and compels us to walk in greater trust
and holiness. This is no passive affection, but a feisty, fiery
pledge to grow us into the fullness of Christ. When we
embrace this love and cultivate an awareness of it, our hearts
are filled with joy.

Such awareness strengthens our resolve that no matter
the fight, we face it confident that God is with us and for us.
When we fight back with joy, we no longer size the character
of God according to our circumstances, but we size our circumstances according to the character of God and his great
affection for us.

Practicing defiant joy is the declaration that the darkness
does not and will not win. When we fight back with joy, we
embrace a reality that is more real than what we're enduring

and we awaken to the deepest reality of our identity as beloved, joyful children of God.

We spring from joy.

The character of God and all of creation is founded in joy. A close inspection of the first chapter of Genesis describes the fabric of creation as knit together with divine affection and delight. Throughout the process of creation, God observes and celebrates the goodness of what he makes. The declaration "God saw that it was good" rings out like a holy chorus until God eyes all he has made and concludes, "It was *very* good."

God's repeated declaration of "good" suggests that God *delighted* in the outcome multiple times. God was so pleased and happy with the results that he percolated with joy. The rich imagery of Genesis 1 suggests the kind of creative high an artist experiences upon completion of a great work.

Another vivid illustration of the creation story is tucked into Proverbs. The personified voice of wisdom, one of God's active attributes in creation, describes, "Then I was constantly at his side. I was filled with *delight* day after day, *rejoicing* always in his presence, *rejoicing* in his whole world and *delighting* in mankind."

In this passage, we see that joy springs from God and all that exists was born in joy. The astonishing love of God found in the relational dance of the Trinity is brimming with delight. Joy splashes at Jesus' baptism as the Holy Spirit descends and the Father proclaims Christ as his beloved Son, with whom he is "well pleased." The fullness of joy abides in God's presence.

We are created for joy.

Just as the life of God is characterized by joy, those created in God's image are imbued with joy. We are bestowed with a capacity to experience joy, happiness, merriment, rejoicing, playfulness, and laughter.

Our world is laced with divine gifts that produce delight. In God's abundant generosity, he showers an array of joyful gifts on all people. Scripture mentions many: a cheerful word, a surprise birthday party, a good day's work, sweet wine, extra virgin olive oil, just-out-of-the-oven artisan bread, sex, the birth of a child, a fiftieth wedding anniversary, the dawn of harvest season, and more.

The joy accompanying these gifts isn't reserved only for followers of Jesus. Many who have not experienced redemption discover joy in all these and more. God is so generous that his goodness extends to all humanity.

Yet Scripture reveals those who give their lives to Christ are promised a new dimension of life and joy, including forgiveness, restoration, salvation, comfort, the law and decrees, God's presence, and homecoming.

Perhaps no greater joy has been given to us than through the person of Jesus Christ. Jesus came to take away the sins of the world. Through his sacrifice, everything that stands between God and us is wiped away forever. We bring God and all of heaven great joy when we give ourselves wholly to Christ.

The Son of God crashed into our world with an angel broadcasting, "I bring you good news of great joy which will be for all the people." Before leaving our world, Jesus endows the disciples with the promise, "These things I have spoken to you so that My joy may be in you, and that your joy may be made full."

Jesus arrives in joy, departs in joy, and calls us to great joy through fellowship with him. The proper response to being drenched in so much wondrous affection is to bring delight to God by offering our lives to him through obedience.

We are destined for joy.

Not only are we founded in joy and created for joy, but we are destined for joy. Consider the following promise at the heart of the book of Isaiah: "See, I will create new heavens and a new earth. The former things will not be remembered, nor will they come to mind. But be *glad* and *rejoice* forever in what I will *create*, for I will create Jerusalem to be a *delight* and its people *a joy*. I will *rejoice* over Jerusalem and take *delight* in my people; the sound of weeping and of crying will be heard in it no more."

The joyous creating of God continues to unfold. He has drawn the blueprints for an existence with the defining characteristics of gladness, rejoicing, and delight. One of the greatest promises to a child of God is that this life is not the end of the story.

You are founded in joy, created for joy, and destined for joy. Joy is where you come from. Joy is what you are created to experience. Joy is where you are headed.

Joy is your heritage, purpose, and destiny.

Joy is a far more dynamic, forceful weapon than most of us realize. The abiding sense that you are fiercely loved by God? *That* kind of joy empowers you to rise above any circumstance.

I decided to fight back with joy, to beat back depression, disappointment, and even the disease itself with this unusual weapon. I reached for God, asking him to fill me with the joy I needed for the days ahead. This decision turned out to be a choice that changed everything.

But before I could start fighting, I needed someone to create a winning battle plan.

.002 | THE LIVING, BREATHING GIFT OF JOY

THE GLOW OF THE COMPUTER SCREEN pierced the midnight darkness of the bedroom. Leif's gentle snore rumbled like a purring cat. At least one of us was able to sleep.

The day after receiving my dreadful diagnosis, I spent hours phoning friends who worked in the medical profession or had also fought the big C. In my hunt for the finest medical team, one friend offered a helpful piece of advice: "The most important person you will work with is the oncologist." Though I'd be under the watch of surgeons, radiologists, nurse practitioners, physical therapists, nurses, nutritionists, and more, the oncologist I chose would serve as the quarterback of my medical team.

So there I sat, propped on pillows in the middle of the night, sifting through Colorado's most renowned oncologists on Google.

I read patient reviews, dissected educational credentials, and cataloged areas of expertise. One name stood above the rest: an associate professor and researcher who specialized in treating women under age forty-five with a cancer diagnosis.

Her face beamed from my screen. On paper, she was what I was looking for. She held degrees from the finest medical schools in the nation and managed her own research laboratory with funding from world-famous foundations. I needed to know if she would embrace my unconventional strategy for facing this crisis. Would she be willing to support me as I searched for ways to fight back with joy?

I scheduled an appointment to find out.

The morning of our meeting, before I finished dressing, I popped the top off a black Magic Marker and jotted a cheeky joke across my breast. A mischievous grin stretched across my face as I buttoned my blouse and shouted to Leif that I was ready.

The nurse ushered us into the procedure room where the smell of disinfectant wafted in the air. We waited for the oncologist's arrival. Leif rubbed my back as I closed my eyes, taking a series of calming breaths. If time hurried, maybe my nerves would stop feeling like fiery metal springs.

The sound of the door cracking startled me. My back stiffened. A confident woman with chestnut hair entered the room, greeting us with a strong handshake. Without the slightest hint of being in a hurry, she explained the test results from the biopsy and outlined a plan for treatment. She shared hot-off-the-press information from the latest medical studies.

In addition to being brilliant and well studied, she dispensed the right dose of compassion. This doctor managed to find subtle ways to affirm my humanity and hers. It shone when she stopped to pet our dog, Hershey, as we talked, and in the hug she offered even though I didn't feel like getting one. These subtle actions reminded me that we were in this together—no matter what might come—in ways that words could never capture.

She shared difficult news without panic and provided optimistic news with caution. Her aptitude to remain even-keeled made me not just like her but trust her. As if in response to her measured presence, my muscles relaxed and breathing eased.

I peppered her with questions for the next hour. She never ruffled. I appreciated that she didn't hesitate to admit what she didn't know—what no doctor could know—about the fight that lay ahead. She refused to sugarcoat the toughness of the next eighteen months of our lives, explaining in gritty detail the upcoming procedures.

The moment of truth came: the examination.

The instant she drew back the thin blue hospital gown, her head tilted to the side, with one eyebrow raised. She inched forward, straining to read my poor penmanship.

A grin cracked on her face. And then it widened. And then her teeth spread into in a full smile. And she began to laugh. *Victory!*

Walking out of her office, I knew that I had found the person to lead the fight. Her gusty laughter signaled she was willing to fight back with joy alongside me. Even in the face of darkness, she held on to humor. She would mastermind the medical strategy as I chose to fight back with joy.

"That woman is going to be my general," I said to Leif. "No, she will be my queen. That's what I will nickname her: 'The Queen.'"

The label seemed fitting enough, because I knew before her I would live or die.

One well-meaning friend attempted to correct my reasoning later: "No, it's before God that you live or die."

"That may be true," I said. "But it sure feels like The Queen can make that timeline shorter by what she chooses to do or leave undone."

Leif and I soon engaged in some of the most difficult, sobering conversations of our lives with The Queen. *What are the odds of recurrence? What is my life expectancy? How will each medical decision affect quantity as well as quality of life?*

No matter how dark the question, The Queen punctuated her answers with hope and, at appropriate moments, humor.

The practice of scrawling silly jokes on my chest soon became a litmus test, determining whether a doctor was right for me or not. The first surgeon I met spoke in complicated medical jargon. With some effort I broke through the technical language barrier, but when she stared stone-faced at my inky attempt at humor, I knew I needed to keep looking.

The second surgeon was the complete opposite. She spoke at a street level I could grasp and burst out laughing at the hieroglyphics under my hospital gown. On the drive home, I raved to Leif about how much I liked her.

"Did you notice her name?" he asked.

"No," I admitted.

"Her name was Joyce Moore," Leif replied.

"So?"

"Don't you see it? Your surgeon's name is Joyssss More," he said, stretching out the "s" in her first name. "Her name declares More Joy!"

I sat wonderstruck.

These were among the first signs God was not just with us in this journey, but he was going before us, braiding together the people to advise us, partner with us, and laugh with us.

In the early days of my fight, The Queen and Joyce Moore weren't the only ones on our team.

Friends promised to stick by us, readers rallied, and key people reminded us they were petitioning God on our behalf every day. My friend, Jonathan, sent a ridiculous pair of unicorn slippers so I could chuckle in the mornings. One pastor, Ray, mailed an honorarium check to *not* speak at his next conference. The contract required me to remain home and rest. My friend, Carolyn, sent me a dozen shimmery red Mylar balloons with a note that said she was fighting back with joy beside me. Unbelievably, they remained aloft for nearly six weeks.

People mailed us gift cards so we could swing by an organic grocery store on the way home from the hospital and slipped us cash to purchase medical supplies and inch down mounting hospital bills. Leif's swim team rallied to provide groceries and movie tickets for a much-needed date night. One aunt texted me beautiful photos almost every day; another sent a bizarre description of the size of a cow tongue that made me giggle.

Love flooded our hearts and did what love organically does—heal. Their gift of presence signified these friends were with me and for me, and not because I had anything to offer. No, the opposite was true: they loved me though I had nothing.

**In the fights of life, people can be conduits
of great joy and deep refreshment.**

Though I was tempted to withdraw and hide from everyone, surrounding myself with people who showed themselves safe and compassionate breathed joy into my dry bones. They provided reasons to laugh. They lifted me with their generosity. Their acts of love distracted me from the darkness and reoriented me toward hope. They became incarnate reminders of God's fierce love.

Friends are living, breathing gifts of joy.

One of the smallest books of the Bible reminds us of the importance of relationships. Paul's short epistle to Philemon is closely associated with the book of Colossians. While the apostle's letter to the Colossians was sent to the church in general, his letter to Philemon is directed toward one member.

Before addressing the main reason for the correspondence—to ask for the freedom and forgiveness of a runaway slave named Onesimus—in his letter to Philemon, whom he appears to know well, Paul revels in Philemon's friendship and faithfulness.

"Your love has given me *great joy* and encouragement, because you, brother, have refreshed the hearts of the Lord's people."

Throughout his travels, Paul undoubtedly interacted with thousands of people. Some were unforgettable for their rabble-rousing, belligerence, and badmouthing. Others were distinguished by their kindness, loyalty, and generosity.

Writing from a cold, dank prison cell, Paul ranks Philemon as among the best kind of people to encounter—someone who steeps others in courage and hope.

We don't know what Philemon did to make such an impact on Paul or the fledgling church. Was it a particular act? A character trait that Philemon exuded? Paul doesn't say. But we do know that Philemon brought joy to a desperate situation.

In fact, Philemon's love didn't just bring Paul joy; Paul said it elicited *great joy* and encouragement within him.

Some might think that Philemon must have been one of those boisterous types who was often the center of attention. But the kind of joy Paul attributes to Philemon doesn't fade with the spotlight. Rather, Philemon's expressions of tangible love brought cool refreshment to those he encountered.

Whatever Philemon's disposition, he became a source of *paraklesis*, a Greek word meaning "encouragement" or "comfort." Paul's resolve was strengthened through the friendship. This was most likely a two-way street for the church leaders. Through the time they spent together, Philemon and Paul bolstered courage and brought comfort. So much so that distance could not break their bond. Just the thought of their friendship ignited a spark of sincere gratitude in Paul's heart.

Philemon's influence went beyond Paul and "refreshed the hearts" of the "Lord's people." The word "refreshed" in this verse comes from the Greek word *anapauo,* which suggests calming someone who has become disturbed or replenishing someone by giving comfort. Paul uses this same word four times throughout his letters to describe those who replenished his spirit during ministry.

Often when we think about refreshment, we think about activities that breathe life into our weary bones. That much-needed nap. Those few hours at the spa. The afternoon by the pool. But it's not just activities that refresh us. People replenish us. That friend who is slow to speak but quick to listen. That person who doesn't want to fix you as much as care for you. The relationship where you can simply be yourself. The companion who has mastered the art of speaking truth in love. People who cheer you up and cheer you on can be like life-saving medicine.

That replenishment goes deep. When Paul says Philemon refreshed the "hearts" of God's people, the Greek word used is *splanchna,* meaning "bowels." In the ancient world, the bowels were believed to be the seat of our most passionate emotions, the underground of our inner feelings. This is emotionally charged language. In essence, Paul is saying that Philemon's love affects people at their cores in the most profound and powerful way.

These are the choice words Paul uses to describe Philemon. This is not flattery but sincere gratitude. They highlight Philemon's character and his effect on those around him.

Paul had a remarkable friend. Someone who stood by him on the battlefield of life. Someone he could call on in a time of need. Someone who reminded him that he was fiercely loved.

We need people who will reach out and hold our hands whenever we find ourselves walking in the dark. People who are quick to put our hearts at ease and swift to remind us how much we are loved. These are the friends who refresh us deep down when we need it most.

These relationships are gifts worth seeking. Developing flourishing friendships takes time and intentionality, but these become the people who ground us and keep us going. They become peepholes through which we glimpse the kingdom of God, inspiration to become the best possible versions of ourselves even in the most difficult circumstances.

For me, true refreshers didn't sympathize with the burden, or worse, add to it; but rather, they entered in and did the hard work of carrying the weight. They included April, who accompanied me on doctor-prescribed walks. Shelley, who prayed for me each morning. Kara, who came with me to key doctor appointments. Carol and Marty, who stood by ready to do anything we needed. They provided the gift of their presence and in the process gave me glimpses into the holy.

In the battles of your life, who fights with you? Who is your Queen? Your Joyce Moore? Your grocery-buying swim team? Who is your Philemon?

The Great Joy Giver is parachuting people into your life to remind you that you are not alone. Perhaps you've been distracted by those who have vanished. Or maybe you've dismissed those who have reached out to help. Could it be time to open your eyes and heart to those God has sent? To embrace the joy waiting in their presence? To lay hold of the connection that emerges from being in the foxhole together?

I think of a woman named Judy, who became too ill to attend a weekend retreat where I was speaking. Her closest friends didn't want her to miss a moment of the event, but bringing home recordings of the sessions wasn't enough. They snapped a photo of Judy, enlarged her face to life size, printed two copies, and taped them back-to-back over a wooden paint stick. Judy-on-a-stick traveled to the conference with them. Judy's friends clicked hilarious snapshots of her enjoying breakfast in bed, listening to speakers, and shopping at her favorite stores. Judy-on-a-stick sunbathed on the beach and worked out at the gym. Judy's inbox swelled with photos, not of the event she had to miss but of just how much she was missed.

Or I think of my friend Matt. Sexually abused as a child by an older boy in the neighborhood, he spent decades wrestling with same-sex attraction. Feelings of guilt, shame, and regret compounded as he tried to keep his indiscretion quiet. In one swoop, his secret broke loose for everyone to see. He drove home that night not wanting to live another day. Meanwhile, a candlelit crowd gathered in his driveway. Friends awaited his homecoming. Friends who embraced him, prayed with him, and told him how much he was fiercely loved.

Or take my friend Liv. Her youngest son, Brett, was born with severe autism. Unable to speak, this fun-loving child morphed as he entered his teenage years. Just a few weeks ago, Brett attacked his parents and siblings. His punching, biting, and ripping out their hair left permanent scars. Liv doesn't know what to do. But whatever she says she needs, her friends work hard to provide. They continue to stand by her, encourage her, and help her to raise money for other families facing autism within the community. They are committed to fight with joy beside her.

Some of our darkest times following the diagnosis were when Leif and I were all alone. Yet people unleashed all sorts of creative expressions to break through the thick fog of loneliness. One family made videos of what brought them joy—including their ten-year-old son jumping around on the school playground—to encourage us to keep fighting back. Our friend Tracee forwarded hilarious articles she found on the Internet. Together, our friends reminded us they were with us no matter how many or few miles separated us.

Whenever you experience a sense of *withness*—the awareness that others are alongside you—you can't help but experience the presence of joy.

Merrymaking is hard to do alone. Hilarity is best shared with others. Cheer is discovered in camaraderie.

Even if you feel alone, God has positioned people waiting in the wings to spring into action. They may not be the faces of those you expect, but if you keep your heart and eyes open, you may be surprised whom God uses.

When crises come, one of the greatest joys is knowing who is fighting with and for you. With chemotherapy just days away, I was about to find out how much I needed my team of joy warriors.

.003 | THREE SIMPLE WORDS TO SET YOU FREE

FEAR.

The villain strangled me as my first day of chemotherapy approached. My hands slipped on stair rails from palm sweat. Sleep either eluded me or was accompanied by terrifying dreams. Prayers disintegrated into a whirlpool of tears and mumbles.

God, I know you know what I mean.

I feared the sickness I knew would come. The moon-shaped face, the jaundiced complexion. The disappearing eyebrows. The way children would stare at me in the produce section. I stopped being scared of the original lumps from the ultrasound. Now I dreaded their offspring—those residing as mere cells, the brood burrowed in the reefs of my veins.

What I didn't know frightened me as much as what I did. I heard scores of chemo stories, but what about the ones never recounted? The ones too gruesome to say aloud? What horrors might be lurking around the corner to ravage my body?

Leif and I prepared for everything imaginable, battening down the hatches and driving the anchors deep. We shopped for pesticide-free fruits and vegetables. We picked up bags of prescriptions. Knowing my immune system was about to be wrecked, I disinfected light switches, doorknobs, and faucet handles, then washed every sheet, blanket, and pillowcase.

The first morning of chemo, I flitted around the house wishing I could do more to prepare. The fridge was stocked. Folded pajamas sat on the foot of our bed. Even a pair of bright red boxing gloves—a gift from a friend—rested on the nightstand.

Nothing left to do.

I stood over the empty kitchen sink, deprived of the comfort of busyness. A wiry string of spinach dried to the corner of the stainless steel basin caught my eye. I scrubbed furiously. *If I scour hard enough, maybe the vegetable remains and all my cancer will wash down the drain.*

Leif's hands pressed on my shoulders, muscles turned to slipknots. "We will get through this," he whispered.

If anyone else dared speak such words I would have snapped back: *Are we? Are you sure? You'll stake my life on it, but would you stake yours?*

Leif's presence stilled the churning. He slipped his hand in mine, our fingers entwined, as if we were in junior high.

We packed our hospital bag for surgery. I needed a semi-permanent device, known as a port, inserted into the left side of my chest. The tubes attached to the device would thread through the veins near my neck and carry the chemo straight into a large vein under my collarbone.

As we waited to enter the operating room, a nurse showed me what a port looked like. She held a half-inch thick triangular piece of plastic tubing. The diameter stretched a smidge wider than a half dollar.

My eyes bugged.

"Do you mean to tell me that in an era when we send rovers to Mars and we know what Ashton Kutcher had for breakfast, no one has invented a smaller device?" I asked.

"You should have seen the ones from twenty years ago," she answered.

Gulp.

After an hour-long surgery, a medical assistant wheeled me into the infusion center, the plastic port protruding from underneath my skin.

Still lightheaded, I joked to the assistant, "The aliens got me. The aliens, I tell you, they're tracking me."

She erupted into a big laugh.

Four more hours passed as a stack of syringes and bags of liquid were emptied into my bloodstream.

Steroids pulsed through my veins on the drive home. I felt I could rip a phonebook in half or smash a cinder block with my bare fist during the ninety glorious minutes after treatment. Then . . . *crash*. A dizzy, woozy powerlessness replaced the initial energy boost. Nausea and exhaustion dulled my senses.

I clawed my way into bed.

To be fair, the principal round of chemo wasn't as horrific as I imagined. It did not leave me with a gaping jaw staring out the window, too weary to wipe snot from my upper lip. My first treatment did not turn me into a shell of the person I once was or land me at the base of a toilet begging God to let me die.

That came later.

Instead, I felt like I'd contracted the flu. Not the ordinary strain a third grader collects from the water fountain but one of the nasty kinds you hear about on the news—like swine or avian. My body was hijacked by a hybrid of aches and pains, nausea, and exhaustion.

When I absentmindedly kissed Leif good night, his lips burned for hours afterward due to the stinging poison. I felt like the Human Torch.

I imagined chemo would knock me to the ground, then I'd pop back up like an inflatable punching bag. Rather than one concentrated, accelerated blow, the assault happened in slow motion. It took days for me to hit the floor and even longer for my strength to return. Rather than recovering, I felt pinned at a fifty-seven-degree angle. I was upward but not upright. My strength plundered. I ached to do all the things I did prior to chemo.

In the past, I wrestled with comparing myself with others—the temptation to look at another's achievements, status, and possessions with lenses that delivered fast but false test results. Now I discovered that the only thing worse than comparing myself to someone else was comparing myself to my former self.

Trying to push through and kick against such constraints is human. Life constricted with my deteriorating health, and I raged against the confines. I created a deficit column in my mind and added all the ways my body betrayed me. The grand total robbed me of joy.

I suspect I am not the only one who feels defrauded when her capabilities slip away. Some limits sneak into our lives when we're looking elsewhere. Perhaps you remember a time before sunspots dotted the back of your hands; crow's feet didn't circle your eyes; your lower back felt no pain. The long-lost days when you could stay up all night without needing time to recover or when you could take the stairs two, even three, at a time without becoming winded.

Most of what limits our life is far more abrasive than those slow, sneaky changes. The accident that leaves a body in crippling pain. The stock crash that crushes a portfolio. The layoff, downsizing, or whatever slick word the higher-ups select to say you don't have a job anymore. The grown daughter who moves back home, grandbaby in tow. What you wouldn't give for One. Night. Of. Sleep.

Sometimes we choose our confines, like the budget that prevents overspending or the diet that sheds unwanted pounds, but more often we awake wondering where the restrictions came from.

Much of my work, my relationships, my life was stripped away. The silly temporary body art I'd scribbled on the side of my breast had been replaced by indelible scars.

How do I find joy in this?

I bet the apostle Paul could empathize. This was a man who lived on the brink of death. Multiple beatings left him in chronic pain. Shipwrecked not once, not twice, but three times. He endured toil and hardship, cold and exposure. And he did it all with a "thorn in the flesh." Perhaps a mysterious illness? Crushing migraines? An eye disease? Multiple sclerosis? Malaria? A herniated disc? We don't know.

Paul feels the sting of prison's limitations—the tasks he was able to do before confinement—and likely wonders if freedom will ever come. Yet even in shackles, Paul encourages the Philippians to lay hold of an inner exuberance that transcends circumstances.

His letter to the church at Philippi abounds with spine-tingling delight. Paul uses the word *joy* almost two dozen times. *What is this man's secret? What does he know that eludes me on my darkest days?*

Tucked into the closing chapter of his dispatch on joy, Paul writes, "I rejoiced greatly in the Lord that at last you renewed your concern for me. Indeed, you were concerned, but you had no opportunity to show it. I am not saying this because I am in need, for I have learned to be content whatever the circumstances. I know what it is to be in need, and I know what it is to have plenty. I have learned the secret of being content in any and every situation, whether well fed or hungry, whether living in plenty or in want. I can do all this through him who gives me strength."

This deserves a nomination as the worst thank-you note ever. Paul could have expressed gratitude for the mission money and then darted on. Instead, he wants the Philippians to understand that he would fare well with or without their gift. Even when expressing thanks, Paul intends to teach this church (and us) a deeper lesson about a contented life.

If Paul cracked the cryptic code to being content, then why doesn't he spell it out? What is this hidden truth he keeps classified? I had to reread the passage dozens of times to see through the camouflage right before my eyes.

Paul isn't defined by the additions or subtractions in his life. Whether he feasts on fine foods or his belly grumbles makes no difference. The quality of his day doesn't hinge on sleeping on a feather bed or on a grimy floor.

"I have learned the secret of being content in any and every situation, *whether well fed or hungry, whether living in plenty or in want.*"

For Paul, accepting his circumstances is the secret to being content in them. Such relinquishment frees Paul to glue his attention to the opportunities before him rather than focus on that which has been stripped away.

The journey to joy begins with acceptance.

We tend to resist that which inhibits us. We pull away—physically, emotionally, spiritually—or simply deny the existence of hardship. Worse, we spin in the comparison trap of what our lives used to be. None of these leads to the contentment Paul describes. Such ongoing resistance handcuffs us to pain and unhealthy habits as we focus on the negative experience.

Acceptance acknowledges our helplessness and requires us to loosen our grip, slow our pace, and reorient our focus on God in the situation. Paul does not find contentment in bucking his circumstances but in surrendering control of them.

The journey to joy advances through adaptability.

Once Paul accepts his situation, then he adapts to it. He can rise above because circumstance no longer masters him.

Paul could have beat his head on prison bars or given up on helping the churches. Instead, Paul does something courageous—he adapts. No longer able to travel to the fledgling congregations in person, he sends letters.

Within the ancient world, the price of ink and papyrus as well as the difficulty of delivery made these written expressions a valuable gift. Such letters were considered a manifestation of the physical presence of the person writing. The messengers who delivered them gave updates to the recipients and helped communicate the sender's sentiments. A personal appearance by the sender was most desired, as Paul expresses many times, but a letter was the next best option.

Paul never expected that the words he penned would skip like rocks for thousands of years. We owe the existence of the majority of the New Testament to this man's ability to adapt. Through it, he changed the course of history.

We rarely choose what is subtracted from our lives, but we can choose how we respond. How we reorganize our lives in order to move forward.

The journey to joy leads us to greater dependence on Christ.

Paul concludes, "I can do all this through him who gives me strength."

If we stop after accepting and adapting, we leave out the most crucial element. Our constrictions may worsen. Aging cannot be reversed, illnesses often compound, and financial constraints tend to tighten. But Paul's words brim with hope.

When he pens "content" in his letter, Paul uses the Greek word *autarkes*, a term used by Stoic philosophers that means "self-sufficient." Paul isn't suggesting that he derives satisfaction from himself but, rather, from Christ. Whenever we turn to Jesus as our source of strength, we don't lean on the wobbly crutch of self.

We were not designed to fly solo, to face limitations alone. In fact, we *shouldn't*. Only through Christ can we find joy in the midst of them.

In weakness and limits, Paul discovers Christ as the source of his strength. Paul wants us to walk in the confidence that God is our Tower of strength when we feel toppled. Our Advocate when we feel abandoned. Our Comforter when we feel crushed. Our Grace Giver when the thorn in our flesh won't budge.

The severity of our hardship increases our opportunity to depend on God. In those moments divine grace seeps through the ruins, softens our wills, and takes us to deeper places than we could venture on our own. Our weaknesses become ripe opportunities for his infinite power to be displayed. We radiate God's glory.

Prison guards shackled Paul's body, but not the spirit of Christ living in him. With feeble and calloused hands, he clutched joy.

And we can too.

With each treatment, I missed my former life more and struggled to embrace my new normal. I solicited the help of a wise, Christian counselor to understand how to begin the process.

"I can accept that I'm battling cancer," I told him. "But I don't accept the cancer if that means allowing any of those renegade cells to live in my body. I want it gone, gone, gone."

"No one is asking you to accept the cancer in your body. No, we want you to fight, fight, fight," the counselor corrected. "But to move forward you need to accept that your life has changed. It's never going to look the same. Some of the things you once did may be impossible for a while or ever again. Through acceptance, you will uncover new opportunities."

I returned home that afternoon to dirty clothes piled on our bedroom floor. Everything in me wanted them clean. I knew my to-do list needed trimming. I stared at the colorful clump.

"Accept," I whispered. "Accept."

In those choice syllables, I granted myself permission to leave the laundry undone. Gradually, one little choice after another, I began to give myself the time and space I needed to be sick and allow my body to heal.

I slipped into the pajamas I'd worn the night before and slinked into bed. Somehow I hadn't just accepted; I'd also adapted. In my old life, I would have insisted on fresh, hot-out-of-the-dryer jammies after a long day. Now any pair would do.

Following this path of acceptance and adaptation, I realized that stepping into this new life was teaching me to depend on God. My mind quieted. The last thing I remember before falling asleep to the white noise of the air conditioner was feeling, well . . . happy.

When life begins to shrink, opportunities for joy are magnified.

It seems counterintuitive that less translates to more, but when you have fewer resources—less time, less energy, less of you—you are forced to reorder priorities. I had spent much of my life concerned with the nonessentials, the trivial.

When you can't stand upright and have a narrow emotional bandwidth, most everyday activities need to be reassessed. *And* is replaced by *or*. My to-do list no longer consisted of catching up on e-mail and bathing the dog and calling someone back, but answering e-mails *or* washing the dog *or* returning a phone call. I could only pick one. Once I chose to accept this, I began assessing which was most important.

Some days the priority became eating a hot meal; other days, sleeping in clean pajamas mattered most. I didn't always make the best choice, but I became more intentional.

Perhaps like me, you have a natural bent to kick against or resist limitations. On the day you discover the rickety bridge to your old life is destroyed, consider pulling out a scrap of paper. Create your own permission slip for joy. Write three words:

Accept. Adapt. Depend.

Carry this permission slip with you. Tell your friends you're working on becoming more content, more joyful. Take a nap. Live with a messy house for a time. Order takeout. File an extension on your taxes. Stare out the window. Linger in the company of a friend. Breathe in the fullness of life. Use those words to fight back with joy.

Know that even within the limits, great joy is waiting to be unleashed.

This practice revealed how much, in my previous life, I exerted enormous amounts of energy over less important tasks: A clean house. Making sure dinner was timed well when guests arrived. Worrying about what so-and-so thought or how I was perceived. Concerns over leaving dog poop in the grass (sorry, neighbors!).

As life slowed, I practiced acceptance, adaptation, and dependence as if they were spiritual disciplines. Along the way, I noticed more pauses that I've dubbed "everyday commas" inserting themselves into my life. Each contained a hidden burst of joy. I played with my blueberries at breakfast before popping their sweetness in my mouth. Leif and I developed a rhythm of pausing throughout the day to sit, my temple resting against his shoulder. Even our poodle, Hershey, was getting more scratches and kisses atop his head. Though productivity and efficiency had shrunk, everything and everyone in life received more attention.

Stripped of my self-sufficiency, I found myself rediscovering God as Sustainer. My next breath depended on him. Upon receiving a gift—no matter how miniscule—I paused to recenter myself on gratitude. Though my stubbornness often resisted, joy crept in.

In weakness, I was becoming more alive.

I had much more to learn. To be honest, this worked some days, but not every day. Fighting back with joy requires a variety of strategies, a wide range of holy habits, and *accept, adapt, depend* were just a few of the first.

And I was learning that chemotherapy is erratic. If I had known the toll those toxins would take, I would never have traveled across the continent so soon.

.004 | THE BIGGEST MYTH ABOUT JOY

SOMETIMES WHEN LIFE stills, I daydream of traveling to some far-flung country whose name I can't spell. I always have been an adventurer at heart and am lucky I married someone who doesn't mind a spontaneous expedition. This longing to travel to new places has taken Leif and me to some unusual sites, including hiking the Scottish Highlands, harvesting olives in Croatia, and sleeping in Windsor Castle.

Right after the diagnosis, we realized that one such trip was fast approaching—a spiritual retreat I'd agreed to lead months in advance. We discussed the risks involved in traveling after the first round of chemotherapy. We talked about how this trip might affect my recent progress in accepting my limitations and learning to slow down and let go. My husband, the sober realist, was highly skeptical. But Margaret, the explorer, won out.

We decided to take the plunge and head to Bar Harbor, Maine. Maybe it was the promise of hiking the rugged coast of Acadia National Park. Or fresh-steamed lobster. Or gourmet chocolate. Whatever the impetus, nearly twenty of us gathered in a nineteenth-century home along the coast to study and explore the wonder of God.

That coastal home was transformed into part comedy club and part sanctuary. We laughed until our jaws ached and gathered each morning for devotions. We played and we prayed. Together, we encountered Christ amid the beauty of creation and each other.

On the third day, we commenced the nine-mile climb up Cadillac Mountain, a 1,528-foot peak famed as the first place in the United States touched by the sun each day. Our guide described the trail as mild with reasonable mileage, something everyone could manage. We anticipated a gentle stroll followed by a delectable meal prepared by Chef Leif.

We embarked on the trailhead in the early morning. Less than a quarter mile from the start, the pine-needle path disappeared into a rushing stream. A few steps further and the streambed crisscrossed our route again. Then the trail dead-ended into an even wider rocky rivulet.

When it comes to hiking, most people cling to the key rules: Never run out of water. Always carry M&Ms. Don't get caught without sunscreen or bug repellant. Stay away from wild red berries. Bring extra toilet paper. Avoid overheating. All of these are advisable (particularly the M&Ms), but for me, the absolute rule of hiking is no matter what, under any circumstance, *never* let your feet get wet.

The only thing worse than the word *moist* is having your feet become that while hiking.

I hesitated before bounding on rocks across the streambed. As my fellow hikers passed by, I noticed fatigued looks on their faces. Sweat streaked their cheeks. Unstable rocks rotated underneath them. Some struggled to keep their balance. A few stumbled into the water.

The terrain worsened, slowing our pace.

According to our guide, a healthy hiking rate on the path was about three miles an hour. We were averaging less than one.

Two members recognized the steepness as too much for them and took a side trail to the bottom of the mountain. The rest of the group, including my stubborn five-days-out-of-chemo self, pressed on.

We summited the first visible mountaintop. Below us, a crescent-shaped sandy beach arched into the shore. A handful of rocky peninsulas jutted like fingers into the Atlantic. Islands appeared like dollops of lime sorbet in blue Kool-Aid.

As we paused to snap photos, a hiker passed.

"That next peak Cadillac?" I asked.

"No, Cadillac is over there," he said, pointing to a barely visible peak.

At least six mountaintops stood between Cadillac and us. We had to circle a mammoth rim of peaks, each requiring ascending and descending. The distance may have only been nine miles, but the elevation gain was compounded with every ridge.

We continued, the temperature rising with each step.

Though I had only undergone a single round of chemotherapy, my body was changing. Heat was my kryptonite. A warm room or direct sunlight drained energy from me like a car battery after the headlights have been left on overnight. As the sun rose overhead, I could feel my body sweltering, fatigue settling in. I hunted for shade, crouching beneath any tree with a canopy of thick limbs.

My body temperature grew erratic. Fever and sudden shivers intermingled with nausea and clamminess. Fearing for my safety, I scurried as fast as my legs allowed. With the elevation gain and beating sun, the trail that led to the bottom of the mountain could not come soon enough.

When we peaked the next mountain, I scrunched under a low tree branch until others caught up, then popped out for a photo. As we huddled, a burst of wind blew my sunhat over the side of the cliff.

Something about the disappearance signified the group's vulnerability. Two of the members had become separated early along the trail and we hadn't seen them for hours.

Several members were sunburned. Others were running out of M&Ms. Our hike was going awry.

My canteen only had three sips of water remaining—another key rule broken—and I needed to get off that mountain fast. Our leader roamed the side of the hill hunting for a cell signal to call Leif, who had been cooking all day. This ensured a ride would be waiting at the base of the hill.

Meanwhile, I knew I didn't have time to waste. The trail we'd been following was marked by cairns and a few blue paint dashes that pointed us toward the correct path. Waterless, I followed the blue dashes down the side of the mountain. Scared and exhausted, I descended the mountain in a sprint that was more of a continuous, controlled fall. Taking a short break in the shade of a tree, I asked a stranger for a sip of his water. He generously gave me the rest of his bottle, and for a moment, I suspected him an angel.

I continued to run. Near the road a pair of hikers surveyed their map.

"Is this the way to the main exit?" I asked.

They shook their heads and pointed toward the mountain I'd just descended.

That's when I discovered that all the lines for *every* trail in the park are blue. In my effort to outrun the sun and access water, I'd descended in the wrong direction. Even worse, the group followed me rather than the leader of the hike. Now they had to re-ascend the same steep trail to access the correct trailhead.

Three team members stayed with me as we followed the trail to the bottom, where Leif waited with water bottles and snacks. I reached safety, but for the rest of the troop, the trails grew steeper, slicker, more treacherous. They soon splintered apart in an effort to complete the ascent. Some crawled in a crabwalk on all fours over huge boulder fields. Others scoured for an exit trail because of the terrain's severity. One by one, each returned to the main house with harrowing tales of a hike gone wrong along with scrapes, bruises, and strained muscles.

The last few hikers in our group limped in just before sundown, caked in sweat, mud, and dust and desperate for water. That's when we learned the leader had to call off the hike. At the pace the group was moving, too few hours remained to summit Cadillac Mountain safely.

Members of the group were angered by the inaccurate description of the trail. Some not-so-lighthearted suggestions of retribution for our guide included live lobsters with big claws.

With this mess of a day lying at my aching feet, I wondered, *How can we find delight when life unravels? How do we find joy when everything goes awry?*

Perhaps this is the question the apostle James ponders as he pens the letter bearing his name. His epistle would one day be read by Jesus' followers scattered across the region, a group all too familiar with the battles of life. James' letter begins:

"Greetings."

That one word initiates a bond between the opening and the body of the letter. The Greek word for "greetings" (*chairein*) looks a lot like "joy" (*charan*) in the next verse. Not only do they look similar, but both come from the same root *chairo*— to rejoice. This delightful linkage invites the reader into the purpose of the letter: "Consider it pure joy, my brothers and sisters, whenever you face trials of many kinds, because you know that the testing of your faith produces perseverance. Let perseverance finish its work so that you may be mature and complete, not lacking anything."

James makes a startling suggestion—great joy waits in the furor of our daily battles. Though we should never seek hardships or trials, they serve a purpose. Sometimes we catch a glimpse of the divine intent. Other times we don't. The biblical hero Job never did. Regardless, adversity often reveals the inner workings of our hearts. Trials expose our weaknesses and vulnerabilities. They force us to scout for God and rediscover our need for him.

James says our faith is activated when we live alert for God in the midst of hardship. Not in escaping the trials but enduring them we discover the fruit of perseverance blossoming in our lives.

The transformation that takes place isn't just for us. Difficulties are among God's favorite display windows, providing a showcase for Christ and his character to everyone. The apostle Paul compares us to imperfect jars of clay. Our flaws and broken chips become exhibits of God's power and grace. Within each container, God is at work.

What trials are you writhing in now? Where are the hidden blessings, the opportunities for maturation, the holy moments in the chaos? Stop and look closer. Squint if you must.

Trials can become the gateway to greater joy, but these passages are fraught with obstacles. The roadside is dotted with land mines, inhabited by bandits, overgrown with briars. Telling someone to look for blessings in the midst of burden, however true, is hard to swallow and even more difficult to execute. But the spiritual growth we experience in trying times, though often more gradual and painful than we'd like, *is* occasion for celebration. It's not in the absence of difficulties but in their presence that God bestows a mighty blessing on us.

After the long trial—I mean *trail*—something magical and inexplicable unfolded among our group. I'm not referring to the steamed lobster dipped in salty butter that soothed some of the edges, although that didn't hurt. As we gathered, we focused on the day's hidden gifts.

Though we had felt abandoned on the hike, God had been working, his fierce love for us revealed in our conversations. Trish and Sue shared how they'd poured out so much as leaders in their church the past few years and now felt exhausted and empty. They described the gift they'd received as others walked beside and encouraged them when the trail became difficult. Through these simple expressions of kindness, Trish's and Sue's reserves for loving others were refilled.

Tara shared some challenges of caring for her husband, who suffers from a debilitating, mysterious disease. Each step of the hike, she sensed the Holy Spirit challenging her: *Do you trust me with him? Do you trust me?*

Circe found freedom. Summiting Cadillac Mountain was the one physical goal she wanted to accomplish, but as the exhaustion of the day set in, she sensed God whisper, *You have nothing to prove.* For the first time in far too long, she decided to follow God's lead and leave the hike for another day.

Tom had snuck something on the mountain none of us knew: the ashes of his father. In tears, he disclosed how he found a quiet place to release the remains and the anger he had carried since his dad's death.

Through this harrowing experience, a curtain was drawn back as we listened to each other share how God had used the trek to challenge us, teach us, speak to us, and free us. A hike gone awry became the place God met us. Joy stoked a flickering fire that warmed the room.

The biggest myth about joy is that it only flourishes in good times, or that it is only the byproduct of positive experiences. We assume that when everyone has a clean bill of health, when the kids are well behaved, when the spouse is attentive, and when the bank balance has an extra zero, inner exuberance develops most easily. The botched hike illuminated a greater truth:

Life's thorniest paths can lead to great joy.

Someone in our group confessed, "If I had known how challenging this hike was going to be, I never would have gone."

Most of us are naturally risk averse. We avoid that which might harm or injure us. We cling to sidewalks and safer paths. We prefer the comfort of the known versus the pangs of the unknown.

God, in his fierce love, keeps nudging us off-road. He knows that something special—a transformation that cannot happen on smoother paths—emerges along the rocky, unpredictable terrain of life.

I'd have to remind myself of this discovery all too soon. A few hours later, after everyone said good night, I retreated to my room for a bath. The ivory claw-foot tub felt like an oasis of relaxation. I lingered until the water cooled, then reached for a thick cotton towel. Something caught my attention. Clumps of hair lined the drain.

I knew this was only the beginning.

.005 | WHEN YOU'RE TEARING YOUR HAIR OUT

"Some people *don't* lose their hair," I protested.

"You're right," The Queen responded. "But with your chemo regimen, you'll lose it all."

"Sooner or later?"

"Day seventeen," she decreed.

Something about the way she said *day seventeen* set off an internal stopwatch. I longed for her to be more vague, more optimistic.

When the shock waves faded, I hunted for wig stores online. One promised the finest quality, another competitive pricing. It was too much. The levees broke, releasing tidal waves of tears. I slammed the laptop closed and scurried away.

The emotional response to losing my hair seemed disproportionate. I'd been diagnosed, undergone surgery to insert a port, bottomed out during chemotherapy, yet I had never wept like this. *Where is this coming from? Why am I so tender about losing something that can grow back?*

Then I remembered.

As a young girl, I stood on the deck of my parents' sailboat. A stranger strolled by on the dock. He waved and greeted me, "Hey, little boy!" My mom had given me a short haircut just days before.

At four years old, I knew few things to be true. Among them, my name was Margaret, and I was a girl. The innocent words of a passerby cracked the emerging foundations of my identity. I ran to my mother bawling. Fragile and shaken, I assessed that without long hair, I was unidentifiable. I was neither Margaret nor a girl.

From that day forward, I refused to allow my mom to cut my hair short. My curly amber locks cascaded to my shoulders in a litany of goofy school pictures from elementary school through college. (That reminds me. I need to have a bonfire.) Just before I met Leif, I gave into a kind, persistent stylist who wanted to trim my hair to a bob. Through Leif's loving encouragement, the style transitioned to a pixie cut.

The thought of losing my hair excavated deep scars of fear, fragility, and confusion. My hair, a central building block of my identity, was about to be plucked from me. I wanted to run to my mom and sob in her arms.

I shared the memory with a handful of friends. Something about confessing deep pain to others helped me heal. I refused to let sorrow steal my joy. Not this early in the fight.

After a series of measured breaths, I mustered the gumption to return to my laptop and search for *cranial hair prostheses*, the fancy term for a wig. A salon with a wide selection was only fifteen minutes away from our home in Colorado. I zipped over and perused the aisles, trying on various hairdos.

One made me look like the twin of a close friend. I snapped a photo to send her. Maybe some red locks would make me look like Amy Adams? Not so much. What about some bead-adorned dreadlocks? Fun, but not me.

The owner of the salon, Abby, asked if I wanted a consultation about different types of hair systems.

We discussed options and settled on an auburn hairpiece. She needed several days to wash and prepare the wig for the fitting. At the register, Abby confessed that she, too, was a survivor. As she shared her story, I discovered I had wandered into the one store where the hairstylist just happened to be a twenty-two-year survivor of the same exact cancer—something that rarely happens.

God's goodness and provision were unmistakable.

During the first days in Maine, I'd noticed extra hairs in the shower, but by the last night in that white claw-foot bathtub, the tresses fell in thick clumps. By the time I arrived home, I was patting down my head as if to tell the strands to stay put every day. Yet they fell everywhere. Stray hairs appeared all over my pillow, even on my dinner plate. One afternoon, I glanced down at Hershey nestled on my lap. Instead of finding dog hair on me, I had shed all over the dog.

My scalp throbbed. No one told me to expect pain. The touch of my head against the pillow evoked a sharp twinge. I attempted to sleep facedown—an impossible task. The slightest gust of wind incited agony as locks fluttered away.

By fateful day seventeen, I could no longer cling to my strands. Sitting in Abby's chair, I examined my scalp. Much of my hair dislodged from the follicle and barely held on.

"Are you ready?" Abby asked, gripping a buzzing pair of hair clippers.

"Wait," I said. "Can I pull it out?"

"Sure. I'll give you a minute."

I can't pinpoint what spurred the desire. At the hospital I was a willing subject for poking, prodding, and poisoning. Perhaps this was the only opportunity where I could hold the reins of my suffering. I refused to let it pass.

Lifting my hand, I grasped a tuft just above my forehead. I felt the follicles give. Clumps dropped to the ground. The slightest tug removed handfuls of hair. The process did not carry physical pain anymore, but each pull provided an emotional release.

Until this moment, I never considered the role hair plays in the expression of emotion. People touch, comb, or braid each other's hair as a sign of affection or companionship. In India, an age-old expression translates, "I grew so frustrated, I plucked the hair off my head." In America, we use a similar phrase: wanting to "tear our hair out."

As the tresses amassed at my feet, my mind wandered to the Nazirites, who shaved their head as a sign of dedication to God, and then to the Old Testament prophets Ezra and Jeremiah, for whom plucking hair was an expression of mourning.

The furor of my medical treatment left little time for grieving the innumerable losses. My limited energy reserves were dedicated to enduring, persevering, inching forward on scraped-up elbows through the dark tunnel that lay ahead. Yet in a salon chair I stumbled into a grace-filled moment of mourning.

The hairs abandoned their posts until my feet were buried. When the tresses stopped tumbling, only a thin coverage remained.

"You can shave now."

The prongs of the razor felt cool against my scalp. Staring in the mirror, I watched a stranger emerge. When Abby finished, only a stubby layer of peach fuzz remained. I inspected my head, searching for a hidden giraffe-shaped birthmark or a long-forgotten scar from childhood. No such luck.

If I had to be bald, I determined to become a classy bald. What I didn't realize that day, and would only learn through others, is the secret gift of losing one's hair: it highlights a person's most beautiful features.

We all have moments when we want to tear our hair out. Maybe you've never yanked hair from your crown, but you have encountered situations where your children or your spouse or your boss or your parents made you want to pull out your hair. Exasperated, you would do anything to regain control, even for a sliver of time.

When everything goes awry, we are tempted to rush past, stuff, deny, or file the situation under "unmentionables." We will do anything to make the chaos subside. Something inside us lunges to grieve, but we stiff-arm the impulse, forcing ourselves to keep it together.

I knew I needed to mourn, but I struggled to allow the tears to flow. I had committed to fight back with joy. Wasn't bereavement the antithesis of joy? Stumbling across the words of Jesus in one of his most famous sermons, I spotted something I'd never noticed.

Unlike Matthew, who describes Jesus ascending a mountain to address the people, Luke places Jesus in the center of the crowd. He steps among the mentally ill, those crippled by infirmity, people barely hanging on to life. Rubbing elbows with those who have diseases and unclean spirits, Jesus tells them to consider themselves blessed:

"You are blessed when the tears flow freely. Joy comes with the morning."

The Greek word for "blessed" is *makarios* and can be translated "happy" or "fortunate." Jesus describes the down-and-out as the lucky ones. Such words seem counterintuitive. After all, tears are often seen as a sign of weakness—the crinkly white flag of giving up. Jesus declares that those strong enough to allow the sobs to escape are among the fortunate. The Son of God gives the quivering permission to mourn.

Perhaps we should not be surprised. Many of Israel's prophets were poets. Their stark words evoked weeping. Those tears provided a pathway to relinquishment. Through mourning, the people released the way things were so they could embrace how things might be. They traded their exasperation for expectation.

A friend of mine talks about grief and the process of mourning as if it's a river. He points out that there's more to a river than meets the eye. The river's current smooths the rough edges of stones and provides an outlet for fish to travel to mating grounds. Biochemical processes degrade and decompose organic waste. The rushing water flushes away debris.

So it is with the river called mourning. If you poke your head beneath the rippled surface, you see deposits being washed away that long needed to be released. Sometimes the river rushes unexpectedly, knocking you off your feet; other times it laps gently around your ankles. And if you pause long enough, you discover small treasures worthy of pocketing.

My friend's image awakened me to a truth I suspect Jesus knew:

Mourning is a river that carries us to joy.

Sometimes we need to give space for grief in order to make room for joy. No one is immune to sorrow, and only those who learn to grieve well can recapture the healing it brings. Just as light needs darkness, so joy needs grief. And just as night precedes morning, so joy comes in the mourning.

My visit to the salon revealed a deep desire to mourn well. The process of mourning is like a long exhale. Expelling sorrow can feel like it's emptying us of life, but it's crucial to breathing joy more deeply.

No longer in Abby's chair, I struggled to unleash the anguish stirring inside. My emotions bounced like lottery balls of shock, denial, anger, bargaining, depression, and acceptance. Expressions of mourning came in unpredictable fits and spurts. I wondered if, like the decision to pull out my hair, I could find a way to mourn with more intentionality.

I decided to return to my Jewish roots.

In studying ancient Hebrew mourning rites, I stumbled upon knowledge that would bring comfort for my soul—symbolic actions to practice, as well as guidelines for how to grieve. These practices provided a "theology in action," a way to turn my face toward God in life's most impoverished moments.

The first discoveries pertained to instructions on how to treat someone whose death is imminent. Such a person is to be honored with the same respect, decency, and privileges of a healthy person until the final exhale. Anyone facing adversity longs not to be seen as excluded or reduced in any way.

One of the most painful aspects of my diagnosis was that people, including my closest friends, were already viewing me as long gone. Sometimes I wanted to shriek, "I'm not dead yet!" but feared my words would be mistaken for a bad Monty Python joke.

After a meal with a group of friends, I carried plates from the dining room into the kitchen.

"You go sit," one of my friends snapped. "You shouldn't be doing that!"

Though I am confident she meant well, her words stung.

I know I don't have to and maybe shouldn't be doing this, but that is why I am. I have calculated every last bit of energy this action will extract from my body and deemed it worthy because, for a fraction of a second, life will feel normal again.

I conjured a smile. "I'm a big girl. I got this."

My friends had good intentions, but I preferred when they asked what I needed rather than assumed they knew best. Those interactions preserved rather than diminished my dignity. The question, "What would you prefer?" breathed life into my brittle bones and, in a strange way, issued the freedom to sit back and let someone else clear the dishes.

After the time of death and before the burial, Jewish custom acknowledges a period of mourning known as *aninut,* or "deep grief." These precious hours, often limited because the Torah teaches Jews to bury their dead quickly, are set aside for the immediate family to focus on one task: the burial ceremony.

Reading about this time of deep grief helped me understand that Leif and I were feeling the same natural, physiological response to hardship experienced by humans throughout history. The pangs from trauma, confusion, loss, and dread were normal. Life grew dark and filmy. Something would have been wrong if it did not feel that way.

Jewish culture carved space for these grainy moments. They set apart time for those who experienced great loss to grieve without hesitation or apology. The rites barricaded others from placing expectations or burdens on the aggrieved, thus protecting both the mourning people and the mourning process.

Aninut whispered to me that these times of deep mourning were healthy and necessary. With *aninut,* the demands of everyday life could fall to the wayside. The noisy list of shoulds hushed silent, allowing me to focus on tending the loss.

The unique act of ripping one's garments performed before a Jewish funeral offered something to emulate in the mourning process. The practice of *keriah,* or "tearing," has deep biblical roots. Jacob tears his cloak when he hears the false report of his son Joseph's death, and David rends his garments when he learns of Saul's death.

Within Jewish custom, *keriah* has its own liturgy. The officiating rabbi of the funeral makes a starter cut on the lapel of the jacket or shirt of immediate family members with scissors or a razor. Then the mourners recite the following:

Blessed are You,
Adonai our God,
Ruler of the universe,
the Judge of truth.

Those select syllables carry weight. Despite the painful loss, mourners bless God and acknowledge his sovereignty even in the wake of calamity. This prayer isn't spoken with levity or ease, but rather acknowledges the supremacy of God's perspective. Even when his judgments don't make sense, God remains the only true Judge.

After these difficult syllables are spoken, the mourners rip the fabric of their garments. The dramatic act provides a sanctioned expression of pain and anger, a symbolic declaration, "My world and heart are torn apart by this loss." The tradition validates the spectrum of emotions felt by the bereaved, including guilt, anger, frustration, and confusion.

Following the tearing of the cloth, mourners recite Job's words after he loses his children, livestock, servants, and wealth in a single day:

God has given.
God has taken.
Blessed be the name.

Tears welled as I reflected on these words. The beauty of the practice overtook me. I had discovered a sanctioned expression of pain and anger, emotions that most adults I knew had mastered the art of muting.

Some take the *Mad Men* approach, numbing the pain with martinis, nicotine, or pills. Others resort to religiosity as if saying God's name with two syllables increases its potency. Still others forge agony and fury into weapons, pointing them like six-shooters at unsuspecting sales clerks, fellow drivers, or worse, their close friends or family members. At one time or another, I tried all the above. None seemed to work well.

One afternoon when the house sat quiet, I slipped into our bedroom and closed the door. Clutching a pair of scissors, I thumbed through my closet looking for a garment to rend. I yanked it off the hanger and pulled the shirt over my head.

Sitting on the edge of the bed, lights off, I paused before speaking:

Blessed are You,
Adonai our God,
Ruler of the universe,
the Judge of truth.

I did not feel like offering a blessing, but chose to anyway. Only after the words left my lips did they feel good or right.

The word "our" reminded me that I was not suffering alone. Such anguish has plagued humanity for millennia. Perhaps one day, my pain would also become a salve to others.

I snipped a short incision on the collar of the shirt. A gentle pull on both corners of the tear split the shirt with a slow *rrrrrrriiiippppping* sound.

Then I turned to the words of Job:

God has given.
God has taken.
Blessed be the name.

Maybe it was my imagination, but something dislodged in my communication with God. A blockage to him was replaced with a newfound tenderness. In this prayer, in this act, I had somehow become more honest than ever with my pain and anger.

My garment rent, I sat half-naked in the darkness, mended in some mysterious way.

Throughout the next few months, I returned to this ancient practice many times. I tore my garments in the wake of heartbreaking test results, in the aftermath of torturous treatments, at the discovery of a medical blunder by a nurse, at the sight of more than a dozen rugged scars across my chest.

The more we strive to hold everything together, the more we fall apart. But when we release and learn to mourn, we discover the truth Jesus promised: "You are blessed when the tears flow freely. Joy comes with the morning."

What do you need to grieve? What is damming up the cleansing river of mourning inside you?

Betrayal? Disappointment? Heartbreak? Divorce? The suicide that shocked everyone?

Sometimes we sweep away opportunities to grieve by convincing ourselves the loss is no big deal or if we ignore the loss, it will vanish. They never do. Some of the losses that need the most grieving took place decades ago. When we don't allow ourselves to grieve well, something inside us dies. Our bandwidth for feeling narrows and emotional signals seem to fade. We may not feel as much pain, but we also don't feel as much joy.

Our spiritual vitality depends on our ability to mourn the notable losses in life—the death of a loved one, infertility, miscarriage, childhood abuse. But it also depends on our willingness to mourn those tucked away by time and circumstance. Sometimes the quieter losses prove to be the most important—the move to a new town, the unmet expectation you've never said aloud, the unrealized dream that haunts you when you can't sleep.

Just as *keriah* encourages Jewish mourners to voice the unspeakable to God, so, too, must we find those spaces and places where we can bear our broken souls to the only One who brings healing.

Where is that space for you? Maybe you need to take some time to find that place of honesty and speak freely to God.

Or perhaps you need to find a grief partner, someone to gently remind you to let it all out. Who will support you in your bid for new life?

Maybe you need to write a lament of mourning or find a garment in your closet and give it a good old-fashioned rip before God.

Life's demands pull us away from mourning, so we must ferret out nooks and crannies of time in which to allow the tears, the emotions, the hair to fall. Some of those moments arrive at appointed times—the funeral, the boss's office, the flip of a cold pillow in the middle of the night. Sometimes we must create them like the rending of clothes or like one woman I know who held a funeral for her breasts. And sometimes we need to embrace the restorative nature of mourning when it comes.

Pockets of mourning soon surfaced throughout my day. I wept in the movie theater during a matinee. The dam of tears broke as I watched the sun beam its final vibrant shadows over the mountains. They flowed during times of study and reflection, on daily hikes, in the darkness of the bedroom. Many mornings Leif and I nestled on the couch engaged in the gravest conversations any couple can have. All too often our words turned to weeping, as we lay in each other's arms.

All those tears were cleansing me. This grieving was washing away my secondhand priorities, reservoirs of ingratitude embedded in my soul, strongholds of immaturity that should have disappeared long ago. Through the passageway of tears, I was able to reawaken to life's beauty.

Indeed, grieving may last for the night, but joy doesn't only wait for the morning—it comes in the *mourning* too. Much like the sky holds both the sun and moon, our lives are comprised of both sorrow and joy. In some seasons, we will see more of one than the other. Like a solar eclipse, a life fully lived will encompass both.

Adversity invites us to mourn. Such grieving demands a level of vulnerability that can make us want to run, hide, and avoid the outpouring. When done well, the tears of mourning become a river that washes away our pain, a holy stream carrying us toward healing, wholeness, and joy.

Having embraced mourning, I now needed to learn how to celebrate while suffering. No one could have guessed what that would require of me.

.006 | HOW TO THROW THE BEST PARTY EVER

IN ALL THE descriptions of chemotherapy I had encountered, I don't remember hearing about *pain*. Perhaps it was an aside. Tucked into the fine print. Whatever the cause, this single syllable leapt from the shadows and drove a knife between my shoulder blades.

Some mornings I woke feeling as if I had been in a bar fight. *Is that a piece of lint on my slipper or a shard from a broken bottle?* The pain was so severe, I lifted my shirt searching for traces of a lashing—bruises, welts, swelling—some proof I'd sleepwalked into a brawl. Though my skin showed no visible marks, the pain shrieked from within.

I asked The Queen why the later rounds of chemo made the first one look like child's play.

"Your first treatment followed the port surgery so you slept a lot, right?" she asked.

"Probably sixteen to twenty hours a day or more," I said.

"When you're not awake, chemo is much better," The Queen explained, her eyes soft with pity.

The pain intensified and varied with each treatment. Some days, I felt as if I'd been forced to drink a gallon of seawater. Others, I felt strapped into a nineteenth-century corset. Sometimes I crawled into a darkened room, begging for release from the drilling deep in my skull. The miseries arrived, compounded, faded.

"Some people receive chemo, take a nap, and never miss a day of work," The Queen admitted.

"Who are these superhumans, and how can I steal their powers?"

"Everybody is different," she explained. "Give me a motorcycle-riding, three-packs-a-day-smoking, gin-drinking woman with tattoos, and she will skate through chemo."

"Shoulda bought a Harley," I deadpanned.

Making medical decisions was like being led to a table and forced to select the revolver, the chainsaw, the meat cleaver, the bow and arrow—not which one, but which order.

En route to the hospital to make one such decision, I stopped to observe a woman perched near the front entrance. I'd seen her a dozen times but hadn't taken notice until now. Tight silver ringlets framed this woman's kind face, her tender grin.

This elderly lady could have spent her days chatting with friends about yesteryear or people-watching at the local mall, but she chose instead to volunteer her time supplying cheerful directions to those needing help navigating the medical facility. Rather than hoarding her time at home, she offered hellos and smiles to those who needed them.

And she did it all from a wheelchair.

Mind you, this was no ordinary wheelchair. It was decked out with pom-poms and stickers that matched her colorful sweater covered in pins featuring hilarious and inspiring one-liners. A teddy bear dressed in scrubs perched on her chair's back panel with a red, white, and blue patch that read, "Smile please."

But a wheelchair, nonetheless. A constant reminder of the restraints of her life. I was struck by the paradox. She had learned to throw confetti in a difficult circumstance.

I felt trapped in a labyrinth of medical horrors, but standing before this woman I wondered if another way was possible.

What would it look like to celebrate while suffering? How can I throw a party in the midst of my pain?

Nehemiah stands at a similar crossroads thousands of years before. He may not have battled cancer, but he wrestled adversity. Jerusalem was razed to the ground by Babylon more than a century earlier and now Nehemiah is sent to rebuild the city.

I imagine his forlorn face as he tops a hill and surveys the rubble. A crushing weight presses down on his shoulders as he tiptoes amid the ruin. This prophet of God, prescribed for the people of God, weeps at the crumbled mess.

I feel you, Nehemiah. You deserve a good cry.

The river of mourning does not flow forever. Rather than give into despair, the prophet chooses to fight back with joy. He shifts his focus, changing the title on his business cards from "government worker" to "building contractor." Nehemiah familiarizes himself with stone and mortar, while his buddy Ezra works through Scripture. Side by side, they team up to restore the walls of God's city and the holiness of God's people.

This is no easy feat. Opposition crops up everywhere. Some speculate the new walls are part of a conspiracy to keep them out. Naysayers tear at Nehemiah's character, competency, and employment history. Construction crews threaten to walk off the job.

And you thought your job situation was bad.

Somehow Nehemiah finishes the project in record time—fifty-two days. The reconstruction of the wall serves as a physical representation of the spiritual need among God's people. Upon completion, the people assemble and Ezra recites the teachings of Moses. The crowd weeps over their shortcomings as they hear God's law proclaimed. Emotions run high; catharsis swirls.

In an unforeseen twist, Nehemiah instructs the people to dry their eyes and celebrate: "Do not grieve, for the joy of the Lord is your strength."

Nehemiah advises the people to hire an event planner, light the grill, and stock up on Hebrew National hot dogs. He directs them to send portions to those who have nothing—the strangers and servants, orphans and widows, even the poor should partake.

Nehemiah knows that when life knocks us down, merrymaking boosts us back up. We cannot continue in any endeavor very long apart from joy. Without gladness, the most potent spiritual practices lose their vitality.

Celebration sometimes requires hard work.

Even God makes time for play and levity. The psalmist speaks of the leviathan, a bizarre sea creature God "formed to play with" or "sport with." The Hebrew word used in this verse means to laugh, be merry, or joke. The leviathan turns out to be God's playmate. This is not an isolated example of God's merriment, but an exclamation point on the character of God.

In the Old Testament, God commanded the Israelites to gather throughout the year and celebrate his wonders and provision. From Passover to Yom Kippur to Pentecost, God carves out seven parties a year. The Feast of Unleavened Bread lasts for an entire week, and every forty-ninth year during the Year of Jubilee, no one punches a time clock, all debts are canceled, and slaves are freed. God institutes a rhythm of celebration for his people.

To our non-Jewish modern world, such frolicsome events can appear excessive. With grocery lists and soccer practices, so much revelry appears lazy or irresponsible. Yet these holy events allow people to taste, see, declare, and remember God's goodness. They reorient God's people toward his presence and faithfulness.

The New Testament is full of jubilant bashes. Jesus performs some of his most memorable wonders at celebrations. From his first miracle at a wedding reception to his finale—the resurrection, which occurred in the middle of a feast—Jesus made parties don't-miss events.

How does the Bible conclude? A giant dinner party where we all worship Christ together.

God loves a good party, so why do we resist?

The battlefields in life force us to duck and cover in the trenches. As the sun dips, cold dampness descends and gnaws away our resolve. We find ourselves dwelling in darkness, second-guessing if we will ever escape. Partying is the last thing on our minds.

Yet the faintest expressions of celebration infuse us with strength and fill us with hope. Joy begets joy. Even the most meager acts are an outward expression of an inward trust in God's ability to meet our needs. As silly as it sounds, mirth has a magical way of poking holes in the darkness until we see the stars.

Sometimes it's hard to throw confetti in the midst of a crisis. It may feel impossible to play a kazoo with so much discontent. Yet such celebration reawakens our souls to God. And believe it or not, parties can morph into prayers for God to renew our sense of divine delight. If joy emanates out of the abiding sense of God's fierce love for us, then celebration asks us to take action by practicing abundance in times of scarcity.

Even the slimmest festivities of the heart expand our capacity to enjoy and obey God. They remind us to rummage for God in every situation and declare his goodness on the darkest of days.

When it came to celebrating, I found inspiration in my Aunt Lorna. Forced to fight two deadly diagnoses side by side, she still threw more parties than anyone I have ever known.

Every holiday became an opportunity to convene friends and family. Some gatherings were themed, like her ugly Christmas sweater party. Others featured outrageous birthday cakes, delicious barbecue, and more food than a county fair. Once, she even parked in her driveway a food truck that took orders on site. Neighbors who asked what was going on were swept into the festivities.

When she succumbed to the disease, her funeral was a talk-of-the-town gala that included a cookie bar. Her death and life aligned as friends gathered, played, and partied.

Lorna taught me that celebration is a discipline. Sometimes you have to will yourself to do it.

While I wrestled through the side effects of chemo, Lorna came to my mind. *If she could face adversity with playfulness, why can't I?* Leif and I decided to find ways to cultivate the discipline of celebration.

We had to be creative—skipping down the hospital hallway passing out party hats and shouting encouragement might backfire. But we were convinced active expressions of joy were doable. We dreamed of how to throw confetti and sneak festivity along the perilous path.

"What do the best parties have in common?" Leif asked.

"Tasty food," I said, eyes widening.

From then on, we rarely showed up for appointments empty-handed. It started with offering chocolate chunk squares to the nurses, doctors, and other patients. Then soft peanut butter cookies and white chocolate chip macadamia nut bars. Then dark triple chocolate brownies. (We noticed our popularity soared.)

One week, Leif made his famous black-eyed pea hummus with pita chips. Another, he experimented with specialty ranch dip and crisp vegetables. When I learned that one of the nurses had diabetes, I brought her raspberries, a fine accouterment to any bash. Somehow the flavor of joy cut through pain's bitterness.

The simple act of bringing snacks to the doctors and nurses who served us breathed life into both parties. The food created points of connection that humanized the medical staff to me and, I suspect, me to them.

We soon looked for other ways to improve others' hospital visits. Leif collected magazines for the waiting rooms, and we left funny titles on the shelves of the hospital's book exchange. Scouring the Internet, we searched for hilarious videos to show the infusion clinic nurses and looked for opportunities to compliment those who served us.

Waiting in an exam room for The Queen's arrival one day, Leif acted on a wild whim. He slipped into the pink hospital gown I was supposed to wear and sat on the butcher-paper-covered seat.

"I'm ready for my exam," Leif announced when The Queen opened the door.

She erupted in laughter.

The desire to celebrate even affected my attire. The shades of fashion in most waiting rooms are dove grey, drab brown, midnight black. I became determined to look as bright as a carnival. My friend Kendall helped me pick out shimmery tops and sparkly jewelry that distracted from my sickly appearance. Whenever I'd catch a stranger staring at my egg-bald head, I'd wink and say, "I'm saving a fortune on hair care products!"

Did my appearance and attitude make a difference? Just ask Pam, a woman I met in a waiting room. We became like two raindrops crossing paths on a window. Insta-friends.

I'll never forget one of the first e-mails Pam sent: "I just wanted to let you know that I really appreciated seeing you and your husband after a very difficult 'get yourself motivated for another infusion' morning when you were looking so chipper and cute in your hat! You just made me forget all the sorrow and grief of the day before and made me want to put my boxing gloves back on and go back into the ring."

Little did she know that in the upcoming months *she* would inspire *me* to lace up my boxing gloves. When the pain of our wounds cried aloud, Pam and I prayed for each other and shared the mini-miracles of Christ we discovered along the way. She taught me that celebration provides opportunities to forge friendships we may otherwise miss.

Each medical mile marker became an excuse to celebrate. After one big win, Leif and I ventured to an off-the-beaten-path restaurant for respite. Our taste buds danced at the roasted chicken served with potato puree and grilled mushrooms. Though our bellies were stuffed, we cleaned up with a flourless dark chocolate cake with cream cheese sorbet. Holy yum.

Our new attitudes catapulted us forward. We planned parties into the future. Leif had dreamed for years of making the escape from Alcatraz, the historic island prison located in the bay off San Francisco. He registered for the one-and-a-half-mile swimming competition known as Alcatraz Sharkfest, and we spent many months joyfully anticipating the adventure.

As our spirits buoyed, Leif and I realized we weren't having ordinary celebrations. We were throwing the best parties ever. Many soirees are frivolous, but we needed these. Most shindigs lack purpose outside of pleasure, but we had aim.

Do you want to throw the best party ever? Toss one in the middle of a trial. Start a conga line when you'd rather sleep the day away, learn to laugh when you'd rather lie on the floor and weep, cook a feast when circumstances steal your appetite. Make no mistake: Celebration is a discipline. But it's also divine.

Whatever battlefield you find yourself on, whatever rut you're stuck in, I promise there's a way to practice the fine art of partying.

Maybe it begins with a delivery of doughnuts into a tense workplace or surprising a frustrating coworker with a latte. Returning a sharp complaint with a compliment. Handing encouragement to a downtrodden friend. Or maybe it's expressed in your resilient attitude, cheery appearance, or the lighthearted way you carry yourself.

The practice will vary. A good friend recently shared of her young son fuming when she insisted he complete his homework before playing video games. He stormed to his room and slammed the door, only reopening it to tape a crooked sign on his door:

"No moms allowed—seerioussley!"

When Amy saw the sign, she had a choice: to become unhinged or fight back with joy. She chuckled, not just because *seriously* was so grossly misspelled, and decided not to give into her son's response.

Amy peeled the sign off the door and folded it into a goofy party hat she wore for the rest of the day. When her son crawled into bed that evening, he smiled and even hugged her good night.

Gretta wrestled with the depression and loneliness that came with losing a spouse of forty-five years. Her woes dragged on until she reframed her discontent: "I can't believe all we got away with!"

She laughed aloud, her memory flooded with scenes from the rich life they had shared.

Perhaps you need to tear a page out of Amy's playbook and begin injecting humor into situations saturated with hurt. Or perhaps Gretta's strategy offers a better fit and you need to reframe the questions you're asking. Instead of focusing on what's been taken, find reason to offer thanks for what remains.

Streamers stand by ready to hang. Balloons wait to be inflated. The playlist is ready to blare.

What outfit will you wear? What appetizers will you serve? Who will you invite? You can choose to begin celebrating today.

With the fangs of chemotherapy still buried deep, our days often were injected with levity. We could see the stars in the darkness. Light was breaking through. But our commitment to celebration was soon challenged by an even darker night of the soul.

.007 | THE SIDE OF JOY NO ONE TALKS ABOUT

ON THOSE EVENINGS Leif and I were too exhausted to cook, we found respite at the grocery store's deli counter. We became regulars, learning the employees' names and stories. They were generous in allowing us to sample before ordering since my taste buds fluctuated with treatments. The roasted beet salad that tickled my taste buds one week became intolerable the next.

Our dog, Hershey, always joined us for the outing. He sat quietly in his canary yellow tote inside the grocery cart.

After staring into the deli case one evening, Leif and I decided to search the other aisles for taste inspiration. We strolled each row, admiring the new products. Then we meandered back to the deli, where Leif ordered a toasted avocado and chicken sandwich. The tacos beckoned me.

We took our favorite seats in the food court and enjoyed the meal, chatting for some time afterward before heading to the parking lot.

Approaching our car, I sensed something missing.

"Where's our superpup?" I asked.

Leif barreled back inside. He found customers circling a shopping cart with a yellow satchel. Something was wiggling inside the bag and no one knew quite what to do.

"That's mine!" Leif blurted, scooping up the tote.

We had abandoned Hershey for more than an hour.

Leif and I laughed all the way home, but Hershey's disapproving stares indicated he was not amused.

In eight years of pet ownership, I'd never forgotten the furry third member of our family. I suspected it wouldn't be the last time.

Absentmindedness marked our days. It wasn't unusual for either of us to walk into a room and wonder, *What did I come in here for?* Or stop by the store and return home with everything except what we intended to buy. Clothes soured after being disregarded in the washer. Trash overflowed when we forgot to place the cans by the curb.

As if someone had slipped thick, fuzzy earmuffs over my head, I only half-heard anything anyone said anywhere. Poor Leif bore the brunt of my scatterbrain. He somehow remained patient when explaining yet again, "Honey, your sunglasses are on your head."

Some of the fogginess resulted from the chemicals flowing through my veins, but much of it sprang from sleeplessness.

Tucking my cell phone under the blanket to protect Leif from the light, I'd press a button to check the time: 3:17 a.m. The strangling grip of insomnia set in again.

Anxiety and worry preferred midnight ambushes. In the inky blackness, the pull of negative ruminations became overwhelming. Like a toilet bowl, my mind swirled, circling the filthy realities of cancer. Most of the medical statistics were outlining my odds based on a mere sixty months in the future, not the many decades young people hope to enjoy.

In those dark hours of the early morning, I listened to the tick-tock of every clock in our house, stalked by anxiety that filled the spaces between seconds.

When I managed to find sleep, I fell prey to night terrors, lifelike dreams of the disease spreading, of death approaching. I'd wake wet and tangled in sheets, gasping for breath.

Leif endured nightmares too. He dreamed one night of my funeral and woke with the deep pangs of a widower's loneliness.

The nights became a bloody battleground. Though sleep provided a source of much-needed strength and rest for my weary body, mind, and emotions, capturing shut-eye felt like tug-of-war against darkness. The shadow of every negative outcome loomed larger and more ominous at nightfall. Insomnia left me spinning around the uncertainty of unpaid medical bills, inconclusive test results, the next painful treatment.

The chemical-induced state brought crankiness, an inability to remember, and searing hot flashes. One night I ran out the door to the deck. Ripping open my pajamas, I flapped my arms like a chicken to cool off, hoping none of my neighbors owned night-vision goggles.

The Queen warned us the effects of the chemicals were cumulative. Several rounds of treatment later I realized what she meant: the side effects would result in more pain—she just couldn't tell me how much or how long. The list grew to include anemia, fatigue, rashes, extreme irritable bowel syndrome, mouth sores, and receding gums. Even my toenails fell out.

How do you fight hard when you have hardly any fight left?

Just when I thought things could not get worse, the phone rang. Though the details of the conversation differed, the words were all too familiar.

Dad.

Elevated tumor markers.

Biopsy results.

Cancer.

Nearly one hundred days after my diagnosis, my father was diagnosed with cancer too.

"Not my papa!" I screamed to an empty room. Now my mother had to watch her only child and her husband of forty-six years battle cancer side by side.

I went downstairs to deliver the news to Leif.

"I committed to fight back with joy, but this is too much," I admitted. "I've surrounded myself with a team. I'm learning how to grieve. I've worn vivid colors and cracked silly jokes. What more can I do?"

If only I could grab coffee with the prophet Habakkuk. Perhaps he would have helpful advice for what I now faced.

The book that shares his name allows us to eavesdrop on a man who expresses his fears, doubts, and questions to God. From the opening chapter, Habakkuk appears baffled by his circumstances and, more importantly, by God. He spies the rainclouds of trouble rolling in for the people of Judah. The Babylonians have been on the move, leaving death and destruction in their wake. Now their eyes are set on Judah.

Habakkuk feels caught in the crosshairs. From the first day King Jehoiakim took the reins of Judah, his crooked, exploitative ways infect society. Corruption and injustice spread like gangrene. The spirits of God's people are poisoned with idol worship. Their hearts inflamed with acts of rebellion. In their sickness, they forget God.

Though God is slow to anger, he is jealous for his people. God reveals to Habakkuk that the despicable Babylonians will

bring judgment on Judah. The prophet begs God to intervene, but his petitions fall on deaf ears. Habakkuk's bitter cry
emerges as he questions God: *Why would the Lord use evil to
bring about good?*

Unlike other Old Testament prophets, Habakkuk doesn't
speak God's Word to us as much as he speaks our words to
God. He voices our doubts and disappointments. He enunci-
ates that which leaves us puzzled and perplexed. Like us, he
caves in to the temptation to tell God how to do a better job.

Though he is exasperated, the prophet's resolve does not
waver. He prays, pursues God, and stomps to the city rampart
to wait for the Lord's answer. Habakkuk looks somewhat like
a stubborn, cross-armed kid who declares, "I'm not leaving
until you show up and answer me!"

Yet he addresses his doubts and frustration *to* God, not
against God. Habakkuk never tells us how long God makes
the seasoned prophet wait, only that God responds.

God says the plans are fixed. Judah will be judged. The
tumor of sin must be cut out. What appears evil will bring
about healing.

One can imagine somewhere on the wall, high above the
city, overlooking the doomed Jerusalem, a cool breeze from
the surrounding hills rustling his robes, Habakkuk accepts
that God can transform the harshest tragedies into something
good. That God can be trusted no matter what.

After God addresses Habakkuk, the prophet divulges a stunning confession: "Though the fig tree does not bud and there are no grapes on the vines, though the olive crop fails and the fields produce no food, though there are no sheep in the pen and no cattle in the stalls, yet I will rejoice in the Lord, I will be joyful in God my Savior."

Habakkuk raises the questions: *What do we do when the pantry is bare and the refrigerator empty? How do we respond when the source of our sustenance is cut off? When life as we know it is stripped away? When circumstances flood us with fear instead of faith?*

I could relate to the prophet's sense of loss. Abundant life was not budding in me. The ability to rest withered on the vine. Energy decayed. Even my ovaries had gone dormant. Fear consumed.

Habakkuk challenges: we can choose to rejoice when it does not add up.

The prophet's decision to praise God isn't based on present conditions. He addresses God as "Lord" and "Savior." These two designations signify both God's sovereignty—his lordship—and his power to redeem an evil situation as Israel's Savior.

Habakkuk's rejoicing does not center on circumstances; it's founded on God's intent and ability to save. Rejoicing is not a prescription as much as a gateway to possibility. Hope springs when we realize God as the source of life when all seems lost. This doesn't always happen in the way we expect or in the measure we anticipate. But we can choose to find those places where life has withered and determine to praise God.

Leif and I identified the areas where we felt most alone, most overcome, most discouraged, and made an effort to praise God there.

The afternoon I learned of my father's diagnosis, I had a doctor's appointment of my own. As Leif drove down the interstate, I stared out the window. Every blurry tree seemed to be moving in slow motion. My trance was broken by a faint melody, Leif singing an old hymn.

I joined him.

My voice strained, warbling off-key. We glanced at each other during the chorus. I wanted to smile but could not. Little had changed. I rejoiced anyway.

I trailed the nurse to a changing room to prepare for the MRI. My exhausted limbs hung heavy as I entered a cold room with an oversized machine reminiscent of a torpedo tube. My face remained expressionless. I had no artistic drawings on my body. As if on autopilot, I wriggled back on the sled and waited for a muffled voice that sounded like the teacher from Charlie Brown telling me to lie still.

As my body slid through the tube, I understood why so many people have panic attacks in MRI machines. The constricting space, the rhythmic sounds, the inability to move—all felt suffocating.

Click. Clank. Click. Clank.

Listening to the clamor, I breathed deep. My mind drifted.

Has anyone offered God praise in this place before?

I thought of Habakkuk, that brazen codger. If he could rejoice when an entire nation crumbled around him, surely I could offer something to God in this space. After all, I had discovered a valuable insight through this process:

Fighting back with joy rarely makes sense.

Ever so softly, I sang a hymn based on Psalm 103. The lyrics seemed to soothe, but I wasn't *suddenly* transformed. I didn't *suddenly* feel rested. The melodious words didn't make me revived or happier. Yet it mattered. I continued to sing another line, then a third, until a voice came over the intercom:

"Excuse me, Margaret, can you stop singing? We need you to lie absolutely still."

Oops.

I didn't know they were listening.

Climbing off the sled after the scan, I wasn't sure whether I was different or the space I occupied had changed. But I was waking up to the side of joy no one talks about. Joy is irrational and takes hard work and does not always deliver a happily ever after.

Many of us practice a faith that contains the fine print:

I'LL TRUST GOD

if he does something for me in return.

Perhaps that's one reason we slam into a giant speed bump whenever life doesn't turn out like we expect.

What if you raise your kids exactly right, but they walk away and never talk to you again?

What if you wait patiently for a spouse, but "the one" never comes?

What if you give yourself away in service and end up impoverished and alone?

What if you wake up one day and it seems as if God has broken all his promises?

In these moments, Habakkuk's declaration rings in our ears: *"I'll trust you . . ."*

Even if the figs and olives fail.

Even if famine spreads throughout the land.

Even if the night terrors don't end.

Even if the insomnia continues.

Even if the side effects worsen.

Even if I must fight back cancer alongside my dad.

Even if I die.

When I crawled out of that MRI machine, I felt closer to Habakkuk than when I crawled in. I wondered if the prophet sensed the same emptiness in his gut after he rejoiced.

Our efforts to fight back with joy are riddled with the temptation to turn our backs, throw up our hands, and abandon the battle. That's precisely when we need to praise, when our decision to rejoice matters most. Even microscopic offerings cement our commitment to follow God in anything. This grace-given resolve to celebrate Christ in all things is fortified in the storms, not on the still seas.

I left the hospital recommitted to rejoice when it makes no sense.

Leif and I transformed our drives to the hospital into opportunities for worship. CT machines and PET scans converted into sanctuaries of praise. Even the chairs in the infusion center, the place where deadly chemicals entered my veins, became incubators of joy.

Most days rejoicing didn't make us feel better. Some moments buoyed our spirits, and laced us with smiles that attracted new friends. More often it opened a floodgate of tears. Joy is an action, something we can do, regardless of what our emotions may reveal.

Something beautiful resides in a faith that is not results-based. Choosing to follow the apostle Paul's instruction to "rejoice always" is not a cure-all elixir. It isn't a silver bullet guaranteed to slay every monster. Often we choose to fight back with joy without immediate payoff. Those are the days we cultivate a defiant joy, the habit of worship, and the discipline of faithfulness.

Overwhelmed, overspent, and overtired, my shouts of praise trickled to mere whispers. Little did I know I would soon have reason for great cheer. As with any fight, I needed a win, and I was about to get one.

.008 | ONE PRAYER
YOU DON'T PRAY
BUT SHOULD

GOD HAS A WAY of providing not a moment before we need it.

Having waded through some of my worst days, I received an e-mail from my friend Valerie, who had been praying for us.

Though I had received many inspiring verses from people, Valerie's offbeat entry stood out. She unearthed a passage from the book of Judges, noting that this had become one of her go-to stories for life's difficult moments. Intrigued by the unfamiliar reference, I studied the narrative.

Judges opens with sad news for the Israelites: their beloved leader, Joshua, has kicked the bucket. Everyone wonders who will step in and help them fight the Canaanites for the promised land. The tribe of Judah receives the call.

They join efforts with Simeon and his tribe to capture the king of Bezek. In one of those bloody biblical scenes, the king's thumbs and toes are sliced off. The barbaric act humiliates the king as a leader and incapacitates him as a warrior. All those years of removing digits of other kings finally catch up with Bezek.

Meanwhile, the tribes of Israel advance city by city, foe by foe. When the troops approach the town of Kiriath Sepher, a seasoned military leader, Caleb, raises the stakes among his army. He declares that whoever captures the land can marry his daughter, Achsah.

One of the soldiers, Othniel, accepts the challenge, conquers the land, and wins Caleb's daughter's hand, likely relieved not to have to resort to online dating.

After a slice of wedding cake, Othniel and Achsah settle in the Negev—a rocky, desert region in southern Israel where sand dunes are known to reach one hundred feet high. Adjusting to married life is hard enough without being forced to live in an area famed for its searing sun. Cracked skin. Parched lips. Gritty sand in the corners of eyes.

Not exactly the place a young bride dreams of building a life and starting a family.

This is also where we are invited to enter the story. Our zip code may not be in a desert, but sooner or later, most of us find ourselves forced to live somewhere we would never choose, an inhospitable territory with unbearable conditions.

For Achsah—and us—the story does not end there.

The new bride knows she cannot survive in the desert for long without access to the most fundamental resource: water. In response to the difficult living conditions, Achsah urges her husband to ask her father, Caleb, for a piece of thriving land.

Before Othniel can make the request, Achsah finds herself face-to-face with her father. Scripture notes the newlywed's first response to seeing her dad: "She got off her donkey."

This obscure mention contains a touch of humor for modern readers. Like us, changing her situation begins with getting off her tush. Rather than wallow in self-pity or sink into depression, Achsah decides to act with moxie and spunk.

Caleb asks her: "What do you want?"

You may recognize the question. Jesus makes a similar inquiry hundreds of years later. When entering the city of Jericho, a blind man named Bartimaeus becomes the center of attention when he creates a ruckus and ballyhoos for Jesus' mercy.

The Son of God calls the blind beggar forward and asks, "What do you want Me to do for you?"

Jesus' inquiry seems absurd. Who among the blind doesn't long for sight? But Christ wants to know if Bartimaeus is bold enough to ask for healing. Will he relinquish the life he knows for the life Christ has for him?

Bartimaeus does not hesitate: "Rabboni, I want to regain my sight!"

He opens his eyes to a kaleidoscope of colors. The first person who comes into focus is likely Jesus. Even when Bartimaeus blinked, he probably couldn't shake that image from his mind for the rest of his life.

Miraculous transformation begins with one question from God:

"What do you want Me to do for you?"

That explosive query underlines some of the most audacious prayers and petitions in the Bible.

Consider Jacob. He spends the midnight hours wrestling with a divine messenger. Before sunrise, he grows daring. He refuses to release the figure without a blessing. Jacob receives more than he bargains for—both in divine favor and a new name, Israel.

Remember Hannah? Her life is marred by infertility. She fearlessly asks God for a son and soon gives birth to Samuel. This child grows up to become a great prophet and adviser to the kings of Israel.

Then there's Bathsheba. When her husband, King David, asks what she wants, she appeals to make her son, Solomon, the next king. The spunky request not only secures the boy's future but also saves her life.

And Solomon. Newly appointed to rule over God's people, Solomon makes a valiant request. He asks for "a discerning heart" to govern the people, but receives more than he expected. He becomes the wisest man who ever walked the earth and receives great wealth and honor to boot.

Maybe desperation drove Achsah. Or perhaps it was this same holy audacity demonstrated by the people of God throughout history. Whatever the case, Achsah makes a blistering request of her dad:

"Give me a blessing," she says. "Since you have given me the land of the Negev, give me also springs of water."

Achsah could have responded to her father's question with complaints about being bartered for a military victory and forced into marriage. She could have bemoaned the desolate living conditions or the stinging loneliness she felt living in the middle of nowhere.

Instead, Achsah responds with panache, asking for a blessing or, as some translate, a "special favor." She says, "If you're going to force me to live in the desert, give me what I need to survive."

Achsah pleads for a source of salvation in the land she is being sent, in the marriage in which she is obligated, in the desert where she will build a life. She asks for a commodity so vital that thousands of years later researchers still track the levels of morning dew in the region every day.

Caleb doesn't appear to be taken back by his daughter's brashness. If anything, he may have felt proud of his daughter, all grown up, giving voice to what she and her family need most.

In response, Caleb gives Achsah more than she asked for. He endows her with both "the upper and lower springs."

I imagine Achsah throwing her arms around her father in gratitude. Othniel guffaws with joy. The phrase "happy wife, happy life" doesn't have the same rhyming ring in ancient Hebrew, but Othniel must have shared in his wife's delight.

As I studied this story, something surged inside me. The diagnosis exiled me into a difficult and desolate land. I longed to escape and return to my previous life. With no way out, Achsah pointed the way forward. Just as she approached her earthly father with a courageous request, I could be bold with my heavenly Father.

Achsah's petition became mine. Like her, I could get off my—*ahem*—donkey and approach my Father to ask for springs of water.

I was not sure what my "springs" looked or tasted like. But more than anything, I ached for Christ, the Living Water, to replenish me in the wilderness. I thirsted for Jesus' sweet presence and pined to experience his provision in ways that would leave me wonderstruck.

In the desert of despair,
springs of water unlock reservoirs of joy.

Achsah's story serves as a reminder that we can petition God for sweet water when circumstances make us feel like we're sucking sand. In those moments, we can ask for special favor and expect God to work in powerful ways. If an earthly father will meet his daughter's needs with such generosity, how much more will our heavenly Father meet ours?

This isn't a prayer to make us rich or treat God like a cosmic vending machine. Unlike asking God to expand our territory, the request of Achsah is to water the territory we're in.

A prayer for springs in the desert is a request to discover the fullness of life even when facing trouble and difficulty. When Jesus said he came that we might have life to the full, he spoke of that which covered the gamut of human experience—joy and sorrow, gain and loss, pleasure and pain. Such fullness depends on Christ, the Living Water, to grow us in the likeness of God, to expand our hearts, to water our deserts. Our days may not be easy, but they are always full when lived in Christ.

This is the one prayer you don't pray, but should.

Sitting on the couch reading the passage suggested by Valerie, the boldness of Achsah welled within me. I lifted my eyes and prayed aloud:

I'm parched, God. I never imagined this life. I am tired of living in this desert. I don't know why you allowed me to come to this place or even if I will get out alive. But if I must live here, then give me springs of water.

Every day for the next few weeks, I prayed this prayer and the posture of my life shifted with every petition. Instead of seeing only rocks and sand, my eyes widened to signs of refreshment and renewal. Water bubbled up, and I slurped in God's goodness.

As Leif and I approached our ten-year wedding anniversary, we considered how to find cool replenishment amid the brutal treatments. We spent days dreaming about the possibilities. While we acknowledged the limitations, which included not leaving the country or traveling anywhere hot, I asked Leif what unfulfilled wishes remained on his bucket list.

"I have always wanted to be in the studio audience of *America's Test Kitchen*," he said.

The popular PBS cooking series was only filmed in the spring, but its sister show *Cook's Country* was filming within days of our anniversary in Rupert, Vermont.

Really? Anywhere? And you choose Vermont, Leif? We could go to so many other places.

Then it hit me: Neither of us had visited Vermont before. The adventurer inside of me sprang into action. I searched for local attractions, festivals, concerts, and events. With a list of options, one shouted above the rest: Bill Cosby performing live on our anniversary. Leif and I had admired this gifted comedian for years.

I phoned the box office.

"I'm sorry, but the show is sold out," the voice on the line informed me.

I pulled out every stop. Our wedding anniversary. Our first trip to Vermont. A dozen pleas. I even used my best whiny voice reserved for those times when I'm bent on wearing someone down.

No luck.

Having given up, I became unexpectedly vulnerable with a ticket salesman I'd never met: "I really appreciate you looking, and I'm sorry we couldn't work this out. To tell you the truth, I have been battling cancer, and my husband and I really need a win. I thought this might be it, but we'll keep looking."

I scoured Craigslist, the local paper, and even placed ads for anyone who might want to sell their tickets. No response.

Meanwhile, I continued to petition God.

If I must live here, then give me springs of water.

With each prayer and passing day, I heard the gurgles of fresh founts. They took countless forms. I noticed the perfect timing of an encouraging text or handwritten card. Gratitude rolled off my lips with more frequency. My soul found comfort in spending an afternoon strolling through shops with a friend. I was graced with two nights of deep sleep in a row.

The desert did not disappear, but springs were emerging. Maybe some of them had been there all along, and prayer merely opened my eyes to their availability. Or perhaps they were bursting forth for the first time, given by God in response to my willingness to ask. My cracked lips and parched tongue were grateful for the refreshment regardless.

Water bubbled around me, and then our life flooded as if a water main broke. Three days before we left for Vermont, the box office called.

"We have two tickets to Bill Cosby for you," the manager said.

Stumbling over my words, I sprinted for my credit card.

I offered the man a hundred *thank-you*s and received as many *you're welcome*s. Before I hung up, the man said, "You still haven't asked the one question I have been waiting for."

"What's that?" I asked.

"I've been waiting for you to ask where the seats are."

"I'm so grateful that I'd sit on the rafters," I said.

No response.

"So . . . where are the seats?" I finally asked.

"Front row, center."

I squealed with joy.

"Leif, Leif!" I yelled, running to his office after the call.

"What's wrong?" he asked.

"Nothing. Nothing at all," I said. "We have Cosby tickets!"

Leif swept me in his arms and twirled me as if we'd pulled off a grand caper.

A few days later following another taxing treatment, we boarded a plane to Vermont. Though weak and wobbly, I managed to make the show. We sat at Bill Cosby's feet roaring with laughter, waves of joy washing over us as we watched one of the greatest comedians of all time perform.

As I chuckled next to my husband—the one who stood by me and with me and for me when I lacked the strength—I could taste grace. After crying a thousand tears, we needed laughter. This divine gift reminded us that joy is possible even amid great sorrow and loss.

I felt the splash of water across my face, a kiss of God on the forehead. Each giggle and snort was a splatter of holy water.

Another unexpected spring emerged when I realized our lodging was less than an hour from Jericho, Vermont. This remote town had captured my imagination years before, thanks to one of its most famous residents.

I'm not sure how I stumbled on the work of Wilson Bentley, but his story has inspired me for years—so much that I have read almost every published book on his life. I may be the only living Wilson Bentley superfan.

On his fifteenth birthday, Bentley received a present that changed his life: a microscope. This inquisitive young man placed everything he could find from flowers to dirt underneath the lens.

A whole new world opened to him.

When the first winter snow arrived, Bentley focused a snowflake under the microscope. The delicate beauty and intricacy astounded him. Before he could recreate the image in a drawing, the snowflake melted, its exquisite design lost forever.

Bentley became enthralled with capturing these frozen splendors. He developed his own process for photographing snowflakes. On January 15, 1885, Wilson Bentley took his first successful photomicrograph of a snowflake. He was only nineteen.

By the time he died of pneumonia at sixty-six, this faith-filled farmer became known as the world's foremost authority on snowflakes. He left behind a collection of more than fifty-five hundred photographs, some of which Leif and I were about to see.

As we drove toward the Jericho Historical Society's "Snowflake" Bentley Exhibit, I yammered about the details of his work. The gleeful enthusiasm exposed my inner nerd.

"You really like this guy," Leif observed.

"He's my historical crush!" I admitted.

When we pulled into the parking lot, we sat before an old two-story red mill that had been converted into a museum.

I darted past the hundred-year-old machinery toward the back room reserved for Bentley's display. Framed black-and-white snowflakes and ice structures dotted the walls.

Leif stood by as I oohed and aahed and studied every last printed detail about my hero.

"Help me understand," Leif piped up. "Why exactly is Wilson Bentley's story so important to you?"

"His life was touched by the beauty of God, and he wanted others to experience that sense of holy wonder," I said.

Leif kissed my forehead. I caught a glimmer in his eyes, not because he loved Wilson Bentley but because he loved me. Leif knew Bentley's passion wasn't too different from my own.

As our car sped from Jericho that afternoon, I admired the lush emerald hills with ruby leaves dancing in the breeze. I imagined Wilson Bentley strolling the fields, drinking in the stunning details of creation. Who knew an obscure snowflake display could provide so much refreshment for the soul?

The rest of our trip was equally enchanting. Though my reduced strength limited our exploring time, we managed to sneak out for a drive each day. We discovered the beauty of Vermont. We savored ice cream and sorbet at the Ben & Jerry's factory, toured the Rock of Ages quarry, and munched on truffles at Lake Champlain Chocolates. One afternoon, we snapped a photo of six-foot-eight Leif next to the tallest filing cabinet in the world. We even visited a spider web farm.

On our final day, Leif and I discovered that we had written down the wrong date for the taping of *Cook's Country*. We missed the filming of the show. The entire reason we visited Vermont was a bust. But that didn't matter. We drank from the springs of God's blessing and were more than satisfied. Like Achsah, we received far more than we asked.

I don't know what kind of desert you find yourself in. Maybe it's just a dry patch or perhaps it's dune after dune as far as the eye can see. You are separated from the caravan, your camel died, and mirages appear everywhere you look. Regardless, your Father knows your situation. This moment has not taken him by surprise.

He knows what you need and stands ready to hear from you. God is asking, *What do you want?* Will you get off your donkey and ask boldly for what you need to survive?

This prayer provided a change in perspective in the middle of rough circumstances. God did not always answer my prayer in the way I preferred, but he never failed to respond with droplets of grace, splashes of love, and dribbles of mercy. Looking back, I see how the water God provided was the sustenance I needed to survive.

This was especially true on the day I almost died.

.009 | YOU'VE GOT TO GIVE THIS AWAY

In September 1917, the German army released the most lethal chemical ever used in warfare. The odorless substance took twelve hours to take effect. Victims' skin blistered then bled; the mucus membranes around their throats stripped off. What followed was a slow, gruesome death stretching without mercy four to five weeks.

The name of this chemical was mustard gas, and one of the chemotherapy drugs I was treated with for the first half of the regimen was derived from it. The Queen thought that her plan to give the cancer cells a sucker punch needed more than this poison. I started a new drug halfway through treatment.

The vast majority of patients encounter moderate to few issues with this drug. But to date, I had beat the odds. Every time The Queen rattled off the tiny percentile of those who experienced a particular side effect or received certain test results, I ended up in the minority. I was batting a thousand, but only when it came to being unlucky.

Glancing at the full chairs at the infusion center one afternoon, I turned to a nurse and asked, "How many people die from chemotherapy?"

"More than you want to know," she admitted.

My throat tightened.

"How many die from this blend of chemicals?"

"None," she insisted. Before leaving the room, she paused to add, "Because we always bring them back."

If the response was meant to comfort, her words failed. *What did she mean by "bring them back"? Am I flirting with death? Am I going to be writing one of those sneak peek of heaven books after this?*

Though I wanted to know more, I knew better than to press for additional details. Ignorance was far from bliss but better than exploring the terrifying possibilities.

The nurse stood by as the chemicals trickled into my blood stream. I made nervous chitchat as we watched the clock, knowing that those who react tend to do so within five minutes of the first injection. When I hit the ten-minute mark without response, the nurse dismissed herself to check on other patients.

Leif and I exhaled a sigh of relief. We weren't just in the clear; we were hopeful. The Queen said that for many of her patients this drug was easier than the one I previously received, nicknamed "the red devil." We hoped the vicious side effects wouldn't appear with this round of chemotherapy.

When I transitioned out of the infusion chair, Leif noticed a red "O" of dried, chalky skin around my mouth. My lips charred as if I had gulped a gallon of acid. My intestines bloated and boiled. Talk about a sucker punch.

The side effects didn't abate; they only grew worse.

In addition to the skeletal pain, drilling headaches, and overall weakness, a tingling sensation emerged on the tips of my toes and fingers. This strange numbness was soon replaced with a red-hot searing.

Then a new kind of torture: The nerves all over my body flared as if I were being doused with kerosene and lit on fire. I felt like I was being electrocuted. I called The Queen to describe the torment.

"Is this normal?" I asked.

"I didn't want to tell you," she cautioned. "Severe nerve pain happens in a small percentage of patients. Chemotherapy remains your best chance of beating this. Sometimes we just drag you through."

Though I felt gagged and tied behind a horse galloping down a gravel road, I prepared for the next infusion.

When I was diagnosed with cancer, I received a stack of brochures describing what I could expect. I read them all. None mentioned the difficulties my loved ones would weather. For months, Leif stood by my side as caregiver and cheerleader. We had exchanged vows to love each other in sickness and in health years before, and Leif had more than fulfilled his promise. He carried me across the living room when I was too weak to walk and built velvety nests on the bathroom floor when I was too ill to remain in bed.

Leif was a rock, but I knew he needed a break and encouraged him to get away for a weekend with his childhood best friend. My parents could take me to infusion and care for me afterward. He resisted the idea at first but with steady prodding gave in.

I grew self-conscious as my parents sat at the foot of my hospital bed watching the nurse start the IV drip for the premedication. We chatted for the "marination hour," which pumped my body with a cocktail of steroids and various drugs meant to soften the blow of the chemotherapy.

The nurse returned in her Hazmat-like suit to administer the poisonous chemicals.

"I'll check on you in a few," she said, slipping out the door.

"Wait," I protested. "Don't you need to stay?"

"You didn't have a life-threatening reaction last time, so it's highly unlikely you will today," she explained. "If something happens pull the cord, and I'll be here."

Minutes later, pain crept along my lower back. *Must be the hospital bed.* I rolled over onto one side and then the other. Nothing seemed to help. *I've got to start doing sit-ups again.*

The cramp spread around to my chest.

Not wanting to be a nuisance to the nursing staff, I tried to find a more comfortable position, twisting every which way like a half-baked pretzel. Something tickled my throat then throbbed in my lungs. *Cough. Cough.* I glanced down. *Is the skin on my arms turning pinkish-red?*

I reached for the thin cord next to the hospital bed.

Everything blurred.

My parents watched helpless while my body convulsed and the coughing grew uncontrollable. The straining chest pain began to squeeze the life out of me. I could see light but my eyes begged for closure. *Hold on, Margaret. Help will come.*

With a *click-whoosh*, hospital staff rushed in. One nurse slapped the Off button on the IV drip while another injected me with steroids to prevent my throat from closing and stop the heart attack.

By this time, at least six medical professionals, including the doctor on call, were sardined into my tiny room. My parents remained squished together at the foot of my bed, bent on remaining calm.

The coughing slowed, the pain receded, and I regained full consciousness.

"You okay?" the nurse asked.

I nodded.

"Is this what you meant by 'always bring them back'?" I asked.

"We're not losing you or anyone else today," she assured, patting my arm.

I wasn't so sure—especially when the doctor explained that he was going to add more premedication and begin the infusion *again* at a slower pace. The two-hour drip now took six.

Woozy and weary, my parents drove me home late that evening. Without the courtesy of calling ahead, a band of vicious side effects walked in the front door and started slapping me around. By the time I crawled into bed and shut my eyes, all I could see were snapshots of the nurse lunging for the button again and again. I curled into a sickle and sobbed.

Leif flew home the next day. He held me tight, whispering apologies for his absence. I assured him there was nothing he could have done.

I blinked and the next treatment arrived. Leif and I returned to the hospital riddled with apprehension. The infusion nurse monitored me closely.

The first minute of the drip. All clear. Then the second.

My chest wound up in a vice. I hacked for air. The nurse's hand slammed the Off button. The nightmare scene had returned to haunt me.

The staff didn't rush in like before. A lone doctor appeared in the doorway. After a quick exam, he announced, "You can go home. This is too life threatening to continue."

That's when I learned the only thing worse than being in chemotherapy is flunking out.

The Queen called later that day: "I want to try a new drug, but I can't guarantee you won't react again. I don't even know if insurance will approve it. If you're up for it, I need you to stand by and be ready to go."

Sigh.

"Okay."

I was anything but okay.

My cistern of joy had run dry. I fought the good fight but had nothing left to give. Held prisoner by treatment regiments and side effects, my body was giving out and giving up. That's when I recalled some of Jesus' only words found outside of the Gospels:

"It's more blessed to give than to receive."

Paul uses these words to exhort the church elders to meet the needs of God's people without considering their material gain. Though Matthew, Mark, Luke, or John did not record the phrase, Jesus embodied this teaching throughout their stories too. When Christ entered a new region, he offered healing and hope and never requested remuneration. The day he turned fishes and loaves into a feast, the disciples didn't set up a cash register or pass out a price list.

Jesus' declaration of the blessedness or happiness of giving is described in detail in Luke's Sermon on the Plain: "Give, and it will be given to you. A good measure, pressed down, shaken together and running over, will be poured into your lap. For with the measure you use, it will be measured to you."

Jesus is not a sorcerer handing out a magical formula whereby we conjure results because of what we do; rather, he issues a call to step out in radical faith, dependent on God's promises and provision. The verb used to describe what will happen when we give is "future passive"—a grace extended to us, not something we achieve.

Within the passage, the image Jesus alludes to is a container filled with grain. The jostling of the sack causes the granules to settle, making room for even more to be heaped in. This continues until grain spills out all over the recipient's lap. The scene is comical, even absurd. Who pours food all over their lap?

Jesus uses this picture to describe God's ridiculous generosity. Those who imitate the benevolence of God will receive even greater benevolence from God. Jesus teaches that giving is less like an arrow and more like a boomerang. As we receive divine gifts of grace and compassion and joy and forgiveness, we pass those along to others, and they ricochet back to us.

The giver will be blessed! The giver will be happy! The giver will wallow in the richness of a life marked by generosity!

Even with such rich promises, Jesus' command to give was the last thing I wanted to do. The act of giving can become second nature in times of plenty. That's when handing cash to the hungry and lingering with the lonely feel natural. But living openhanded toward others when your spiritual pocketbook is empty seems like an impossible task.

Flat broke in mind, body, and spirit, generosity was not a spiritual discipline I wanted to practice.

If anything, I groped for an exemption clause. I searched for some fine print that classified the resilient and well-to-do as able givers, the powerless as exempt. But Jesus' command to "give" doesn't discriminate. It extends to *all* people, for *all* time, in *all* situations.

Until this point, I'd been asking how I could get more joy for myself. Now I needed to look at how I could be a joy giver. According to this scripture, one of the fastest ways to receive joy is to give it away. One of the best ways to be lifted up is to lift up others.

Time mattered. Each passing day the cancer could reboot and start growing again. Whenever the phone rang, I froze panicky, then darted to answer. One evening, long after The Queen's office closed, I received the call.

"You're approved," she said. "Be here first thing tomorrow."

This was my chance to stop hoarding joy and give it away instead. But I had no idea where to begin.

God, show me what it looks like to give away joy, I prayed.

I thought about what objects best represented joy in this difficult season. My mind meandered through dozens of possibilities until it settled on one: red balloons. They, perhaps more than any other, embodied the weaponry God had graced me with.

Like a fistful of red balloons, joy picks us up when life knocks us down. Sometimes the wall of difficulties we face appears too large or cumbersome to overcome. The presence of joy carries us and lifts us. We become more agile, infused with what we need not just to face the barrier, but to search for a way around or possibly even over that we may never have considered before.

Not only does joy enhance our stride in life, but it also shouts, "Look up!" Imagine yourself holding a handful of helium-filled, red balloons. Feel the tug of the ribbons against your palm and fingers. Notice the way each inflated bulb moves gently in the air. Consider your posture.

Just as clinging to the balloons invites us to raise our eyes in admiration, so does joy. Its presence is an invitation to do one of the simplest yet most powerful things a follower of Jesus can do: look up!

No matter what adversity we face, we can turn our eyes from what's before us and refocus on the God who fills us with joy. Instead of only seeing adversity, we become alert to Christ, who has overcome all things and for whom nothing is impossible.

The next morning, I took a leap of faith and trusted God to provide what I did not have. My joy reserves were at an all-time low, but if I offered them to God, perhaps like fishes and loaves, he could grant me a full belly and feed 4,999 others at the same time.

I swung by the local party store on my way to the infusion center and picked up a bundle of red balloons. Intent on passing out these helium-filled gifts, I approached the long corridor of chairs filled with infusion patients.

A frail woman occupied the first chair. I estimated she was in her sixties—matted silver hair and sunken eyes, but an inviting countenance.

"My name is Margaret, and I've had a really difficult time in treatment. I'm in the fight of my life," I declared. "I don't want to be here today, and I bet you don't either. I want to give you this red balloon in hope that it would bring you joy."

The woman's thin lips curled upward as she extended her arm: "I'd like that."

Turning to the man next to her, I repeated my offer, but with a different result.

"Not now," he said with bone-tiredness, "but thank you very much."

I approached the woman across from him, since I was having more luck with female patients.

"I don't need a balloon, but I do need a hug," she preempted.

I reached down and wrapped my arms around her neck, knowing that we shared so much more in common than geography. The man who rejected my balloon cleared his throat, interrupting our moment.

"Wait," he protested. "I didn't know you were giving away free hugs."

I walked over to offer him affection too.

Next in line was a family of four surrounding their grand-father. Bags of poison hung next to him while his three-year-old granddaughter stood guard beside his bed. When she saw my balloons, her eyes widened. The girl swept her bangs to the side and flashed me a glance, afraid to ask a stranger for a toy but hoping that I'd offer. I knew my next balloon wasn't for Grandpa.

One by one, I shuffled my way down the row, introducing myself and handing out balloons for nearly an hour. Some accepted with little more than a nod. One rejected my gift without even the courtesy of eye contact. A few took time to share their stories with me and listen to part of mine.

The final balloon was the most memorable. A woman from Nebraska received treatment while her husband sat beside her. She was in her fifth fight with melanoma and drove more than ten hours each way every week for treatment. They were optimistic that the clinical trial she was enrolled in might save her life. As I tied my final balloon to the arm of her chair, I paused to savor the way her husband gazed at her with "I love you" eyes.

When I walked into the hospital that day, there was no bluegrass emerging from within my heart, no scent of tulips wafting from my soul. Yet somehow, somewhere along the way, the Great Joy Giver filled me with an unmistakable sense of blessedness and gratitude. As my balloon bouquet shrank to nothing, God filled me, lifted me, and refocused my attention outward and upward.

Joy is a gift we can offer even when we don't possess it ourselves. When we do, something mysterious happens. I always thought of the container Jesus mentions as external, something we hold as we watch it being filled, pressed down, shaken, and filled up some more. I never considered that we are the containers. God fills *us*. Sometimes the effects of being pressed down and shaken around are necessary in order to receive more of the abundance God is giving. The blessedness Jesus describes overflows through, in, and all over us.

One of the best ways to receive joy is to give joy.

Like me, you may not always feel like it. The day you need joy most may be the one you want to offer it the least. Give anyway and give generously.

Take the leap.

Slip a surly store clerk a kind word of thanks. Give that friend who's always down on herself a compliment. Flash a smile to strangers who seem to be having a hard day. A handful of fresh daisies. Some dark chocolates. A five-second hug. Then wait to see what kind of fruit these seeds of joy bear.

By the time I finished handing out the red balloons, I had been inflated with just enough courage to take my seat and face the horror I knew might come.

.010 | WHEN NOTHING MEANS EVERYTHING

A NURSE STROLLED TOWARD ME with five courses of syringes. All had to be administered before the new chemotherapy infusion could begin. As she prepared the needles, my hands trembled. Relieved this was my final infusion, I feared it wouldn't work, another possible reaction, and the dreadful side effects that followed.

Everything hung on the upcoming surgery. Until now, we had no idea if the chemotherapy succeeded. One of the dirty secrets of treatment is that the deadly chemicals don't deter some cancers. My lump seemed smaller to the touch, but I could still feel the curved shape of the hardened intruder.

I endured the infusion without incident. Medical personnel didn't rush the room. No one lunged to slam off the IV drip. I returned home that day to even worse side effects. In a word, they were "unspeakable."

One night a thought passed through my mind that shuddered my spine: I wanted to go to sleep and never wake up again.

I shivered as if a draft swept through my bedroom. It was time to call The Queen.

"This is why I rarely give patients this drug," she explained. "Even for those in the final stages of life, the side effects are far worse than the cancer."

The Queen's honesty provided comfort that my reactions were normal.

While the pain didn't depart, her words unleashed a gust of hope into my soul's sails. If I could just hold on, just keep breathing, I would emerge from the bleakness and pain.

Even though surgery and radiation still lay ahead, each new milestone brought me closer to winning the battle. My body would never be the same. I would never be the same.

I thought of the community of people who had committed to pray for Leif and me these many months. At mealtimes and bedtimes and in-between times, they hoisted our names heavenward and asked God to intervene on our behalf. Sometimes, I could almost feel their requests. When I was drowning in a sea of pain and depression, these prayers became the driftwood keeping me afloat.

"How can we pray for you?"

Some days, the answer came fast: favorable test results, no complications, courage, strength, sleep. But often, speaking about what I was carrying was too painful.

Fear.

Torment.

Agony.

As Leif and I discussed how to respond to this persistent question, one word kept coming to mind: *zero.*

For Leif and me, the number represented our litany of needs.

Zero cancer cells.

Zero complications.

Zero side effects.

Zero allergic reactions.

Zero suffering.

Zero medical errors.

Zero bad test results.

Zero sleepless nights.

Zero night terrors.

We sent the request to friends and family, reaching out through social media to those we'd met at conferences and church gatherings and those who walked with us many years through my Bible studies and reading plans. Men and women who had pursued God with us.

People responded with encouraging e-mails, blogs, comments. Some shouted out on Facebook and Twitter with #prayforzero. A few used old-fashioned mail to commit to pray.

Those prayers sustained us and provided pinholes of light on our darkest nights.

Perhaps the most memorable were the messages that contained only a single digit: 0.

The only number valued at nothing meant everything to us.

By clinging to these prayers for zero, we were asking, "*What if* God performs the miraculous?" I confess the greater temptation was to offer a more vague request.

Most of us discover early on that it's safer to hide behind prayers that can't be measured, petitions so nebulous they don't require intervention from God. Asking my friends to pray for peace or courage was safe. Who knew whether God decided to grant the request except me? Zero carried accountability. We were putting ourselves out there—before God and everyone. The only thing that felt riskier than making the request was not making it all.

If the chemotherapy failed to work, we were warned of the limited options, the shortened lifespan. My last treatment allowed me to sip from the acerbic cup of future treatments that could only prolong death. My life hung on zero like a laundry line.

A Gospel writer tells a story about a man who unlocks the power of that same question. A ruler kneels before Jesus and says, "My daughter has just died, but you can bring her back to life again *if* you just come and lay your hand on her."

Power and prestige mark this leader of the synagogue. The eyes of the community follow his every move. Can you imagine the risky nature of asking a troublemaker like Jesus for help? Grocery store clerks gossip about him on their lunch breaks, street vendors whisper as he strolls by, fellow social-ites cross him off the Hanukkah party invite list. Yet the ruler doesn't wave Jesus into a back alley or try to corner him in the restroom. He approaches Jesus in front of the crowd without regard to gaping mouths or stares.

We can only imagine what this ruler experienced. Who knows how long he languished at the foot of his daughter's bed, begging God to spare her life? The ruler likely summoned every doctor and apothecary in town to test every remedy they knew. He may have started a prayer chain in the synagogue. Exhausting the last resources in his grasp, this loving father must stand by as his baby girl choked on her last breath.

With tears dripping down his chin, he remembers the name of a healer: Jesus.

"Jesus won't come to my house," the man protests. There was a long line of sick, lame, and blind people waiting for him to pass through town.

He looks back at his daughter's limp body.

But what if . . .

"*What if* I manage to get close to Jesus, and *what if* he hears me out, and *what if* he is moved by the request, and *what if* he agrees to come here, and *what if* he lays his hands on her and brings her back to life?"

The asking is substantial, but the string of *what-if*s looms larger. The long line of possibilities ends in a huge *what-if* that defies the laws of nature and pries a child free from the clutches of death.

After clawing through the crowd and kneeling at Christ's feet, the ruler waits for a response. Without a word, Jesus stands and walks toward the man's house, disciples in tow.

Matthew doesn't record their conversation. I suspect the father bounced between the past and present, reminiscing on his child's life, then speaking as if she were still alive.

Rounding the corner to the man's street, the loud cries of mourners merge with dirges of flutes. Familiar faces of family and friends along with lesser-known acquaintances fill the property, but there's no time to fritter with proper introductions. The father beelines toward his daughter.

Jesus flashes one look at the body and sends the heart-broken away with the encouragement: Don't be dismayed by the lack of pulse; the girl is napping.

The crowd erupts in laughter.

Dead is dead.

Jesus slips in, pressing his palm against the girl's hand. With a single touch, warmth returns to her cold corpse. She climbs out of bed to new life. Everyone sees her differently, but more important, everyone sees Jesus differently too.

She becomes a living, breathing exhibit of the power of God.

In the middle of the story of the girl's resurrection, Matthew folds in another tale. Somewhere along the route, Jesus and the ruler encounter a roadblock—a pale-faced woman. The ruler recognizes the desperation in this woman's eyes isn't too different from his own. They're brimming with *what-ifs*.

The woman suffered from a blood hemorrhage for a dozen years. To a modern reader, the problem sounds like a nuisance or frustration. In ancient Jewish culture, the diagnosis was debilitating. This woman was considered unclean under Jewish law. If she had been single, she couldn't wed. If married, her husband was permitted to divorce her. For at least 4,380 days, this woman had been prohibited from worship because the women's court of the temple remained off-limits to her.

"This holy man will probably reject me like everyone else has," she reasons. "But *what if* I find the crowd, and *what if* I manage to get close to Jesus, and *what if* I touch his robe? *What if* I could finally be healed?"

The woman swipes her fingertips against tassels of Jesus' cloak. The bleeding stops. One lunge changed her life forever.

Today, *miracle* is a dirty word in some religious circles. God worked marvels in the past, they say, but no longer. Such displays of God's power are fossils of a past era. The supernatural takes place in other times, in other countries, in other parts of the world.

Anywhere, really, except for . . .

Now. Here. Today.

I don't fault doubters for their hesitancy. Miracles disorient. They shred our theological constructs, our belief systems, our formulas of how we think God should work. Divine intervention smashes these illusions and awakens us to the world as it ought to be.

The more things change, the more they stay the same. Christ's miracles left people confused and confounded, repentant and remorseful, awed and amazed. Thousands of years later, we still find ourselves slack-jawed.

As I was about to realize, asking *what-if* is only part of the story.

Perhaps it wasn't happenstance during this bold prayer campaign that I ran across a man in a coffee shop with an unusual phrase tattooed across his bicep: *But if not.*

Curious, I asked what it meant, and the man shared that the phrase was from the Bible.

When King Nebuchadnezzar II conquers Judah and the city of Jerusalem, he gathers young Jewish men of noble birth as captives. Daniel and three handsome Jewish princes are among a slew of young noblemen in training to serve among the king's court. They move into the king's palace, where they receive new nametags. Hananiah, Mishael, and Azariah became known as Shadrach, Meshach, and Abednego.

The young men spend their days immersed in language classes. They're inundated with Persian literature and the history of the empire. These four friends do as they're instructed with one exception: mealtime. They adapt to the new regimen except when it comes to the dinner table. Why? In part, because the king's food isn't kosher.

They issue a risky request—permission to munch on vegetables and sip water instead of tasting from the king's menu.

While all the other trainees enjoy shrimp cocktails and pork rinds, the Jewish boys opt for a bland, low-calorie, fat-free menu. Then, something unexplainable happens, which under any other circumstance would rank among one of the least popular miracles: the men put on weight.

Gasp.

When the king examines the young nobles three years later, Daniel and his friends aren't only the best and brightest, but the healthiest. The king appoints them to his court. Daniel is chosen governor of Babylon, and Shadrach, Meshach, and Abednego serve alongside him.

All is well until Nebuchadnezzar builds a nine-story golden statue. He invites a huge band, cannons full of confetti, and every "who's who" and "who's that" he can find for the dedication ceremony. The king commands everyone to fall down and worship the glistening statue at the sound of the first trumpet. This aerobic activity isn't optional: those who don't throw themselves on the ground will be barbecued in the king's oven.

Pleased with himself, Nebuchadnezzar cracks a toothy grin when he sees the response. As soon as the beautiful melody of horns, harps, and pipes begins, people fall on their faces, hands outstretched in worship.

Then a disturbing report comes to his attention: three men refuse to bend their knees. King Nebuchadnezzar boils with anger and his face becomes splotchy and mottled. He demands to know why the trio has defied his orders.

"O Nebuchadnezzar," they respond. "We have no need to present a defense to you in this matter. If our God whom we serve is able to deliver us from the furnace of blazing fire and out of your hand, O king, let him deliver us. *But if not*, be it known to you, O king, that we will not serve your gods and we will not worship the golden statue that you have set up."

In response, the king orders the soldiers to douse the flames with lighter fluid until the kiln sears seven times its usual heat. Shadrach, Meshach, and Abednego refuse to recant their brazen proclamation. They march toward their deaths.

Execution by fire wasn't uncommon at the time, and one can only imagine the amount of ashes resting around the furnace. The king stands by, waiting for the slightest hesitance from the men. No one flinches except for a few of the king's soldiers whose sleeves curl and singe when they get too close to the entrance of the kiln. The flames spread so quick the soldier's bodies are soon engulfed.

Nebuchadnezzar, as hard-hearted as any dictator in history, watches as Shadrach, Meshach, and Abednego are shoved into the flames. Whether a hint of curiosity or a trace of regret, we'll never know what compels the king to peek inside the furnace. What he witnesses unnerves him: the three, along with a radiant fourth, perched inside.

Flabbergasted, the king orders the furnace door flung open, and Shadrach, Meshach, and Abednego are rescued from the flames. He reinstates the trio to his service with a promotion.

Their harrowing adventure reminds us that if we remain faithful to God, then he will remain faithful to us and rescue us in our time of need.

But the story reveals something more. Three tiny words: *But if not.*

The three trusted in God's power and might. Yet if God decided not to rescue them, they committed to stand in their convictions.

It's easier to ask, "How will God rescue me?" rather than "What will happen if God doesn't rescue me?"

That's the deeper question that resides within each of us. Eventually we will face circumstances that make us wonder, *What will happen if I lose the job? The house? The marriage? Life as I know it?*

What will happen if God doesn't rescue you? Or me?

Daniel and his friends' selection and promotion deserved celebration. But what about the tens of thousands who were not handpicked? What about those who worked and died as slaves of the empire? What about them?

With the New Testament miracles in one hand and the story of the three brave Jews in the other, I discovered a startling truth:

Joy asks "What if God?" and declares "But if not!"

Followers of Jesus are plunged into this tension between "What if God?" and "But if not!" We have heard the countless miracles, but we also know the stories that don't have an upbeat ending.

Despite faithfully following God throughout his life, the only piece of the promised land Abraham owns at his death is the burial plot for him and his wife.

Moses takes a great risk at the beckoning of a bush and follows God through the brambles of Exodus, but he dies without ever tasting the milk and honey of the promised land.

John the Baptist's birth is surrounded by miracles and the grandiose title of "forerunner of Jesus Christ." His faithfulness is rewarded with decapitation.

Jesus, who on the eve of his arrest begs for clemency from his Father, has his own "But if not!" moment in the Garden of Gethsemane. The next day, he is brutally murdered.

Joy means holding on to hope in God regardless of the outcome. Declaring we will give up everything and entrust ourselves more fully and wholly to the One who holds all things together.

God shows up in the flaming bushes and blazing clouds and tongues of fire. He also waits for us in the furnaces of depression, heartbreaking loss, and a grim diagnosis.

On the night before the first surgery, I lay in the darkness pressing my fingers against the dark villain we had fought for far too long. A wave of relief swept over me. In less than a dozen hours, the tumor would be gone.

As I felt around, my finger pressed against a new hard, round mass. Then a second. And a third.

I froze, rooted to the mattress, beads of sweat across my forehead.

The next morning the medical staff wheeled my bedraggled body into surgery. As I whooshed down the sterile white hallway, my eyes stared into nothingness of passing fluorescent lights.

Would this be the finish line marking the end of this portion of the torturous journey or the starting line for an even more horrid one? Were the new masses thick tissue or something far more sinister? Had the months of infusion worked? Would our prayer for zero go unanswered?

I awoke groggy in a room full of postoperative patients. A blur of medical personnel monitored my vitals. Joyce Moore, my surgeon, placed her hand on mine.

"You did great," she affirmed. "No complications or infections so far."

"When will we know test results?" I asked.

"About five days."

Outside, life moved forward at a winter's pace, but I was frenetic. My cell phone never left my side. I lunged for every ring. No call ever mattered more.

Late on the afternoon of the fifth day, I fumbled for the ringing phone in my back pocket. I stared at the unknown number on the screen before willing myself to answer.

"Hello?"

"It's Joyce Moore," she said. "Is now a good time to talk?"

"As good a time as any," I responded.

"Are you sitting down?" she asked.

My knees bent and the couch caught what felt like a free fall.

"You had a 100 percent pathological response to the chemotherapy," she said.

"What does that mean in regular-person English?" I asked.

"You have zero cancer cells left in your body."

"And the new masses?"

"None was cancerous," she said.

Time decelerated as if someone hovering over me had pressed a slow-motion button. Joyce's voice faded into a barely audible muffle. The room around me clarified down to the specks of dust illuminated by the sunrays piercing my living room windows. I felt like I was in a scene from *The Matrix* where time creeps at a pace that makes dodging bullets possible.

"Margaret, are you still on the line?"

I snapped back into the moment. "Yes, Joyce," I replied.

"This doesn't happen often among my patients—it's a big deal and you should be celebrating."

Ending the call and tossing the phone onto the adjacent couch cushion, I rushed to share the news with Leif. Not a word was needed. He knew the moment he saw the tears welling in my eyes. My arms wrapped around Leif's tree trunk of a body. We lay on the floor holding each other.

We went to see my parents, who were staying nearby. I cusped my hands in the form of a large zero as the front door swung open: "We got it! We got zero!"

My mother jumped with a hug. My dad cupped his face into his thick hands, eyes dripping with tears.

Together, the four of us held a private party to celebrate.

In the days following, I grappled with a range of emotions. Gratitude erupted. *Thank you* seemed like too small a phrase to offer to God.

Guilt emerged when I shared the news with friends—some who desperately needed a miracle and didn't get one. Those whose bodies were being consumed by ongoing fiery treatments.

Fear torpedoed whenever I considered the possibility of recurrence. The tests reported zero cancer cells, but that could change at any time. Cancer is a cruel bully who waits until its prey starts to regain confidence before it jumps out from behind a bush to pummel it again.

Perhaps Shadrach, Meshach, and Abednego felt a similar wave of confusion and apprehension. They escaped the furnace and even encountered God among the flames, but they remained under the rule of a madman. On any given day they could find themselves in the same peril they just evaded. Even if they outlived King Nebuchadnezzar and stayed far away from billowing flames, death would eventually come.

In our journey, we prayed for many zeroes.

Zero cancer cells, complications, side effects, suffering, sleepless nights, medical errors, allergic reactions, bad test results. We got one or two of the zeroes. Most we never experienced.

You've probably prayed for zeroes of your own.

Zero fights.

Zero lonely Friday nights.

Zero regrets.

Zero rejections.

Zero more trips to rehab.

Zero holidays without the people you love.

Zero sleepless nights and worry-filled days.

Zero days of feeling stuck.

Zero insecurities.

Praying for zero is an expression of trust, an act of faith, an expectant "What if God?" When coupled with "But if not!" this becomes a sturdy resolve. The same joyful resolve that traces all the way back to Abraham, Moses, and many more. Each died clinging to the hope that God could do the impossible regardless of the outcome of their experience.

Leif and I had won a significant fight, but we were not in the clear yet. The Queen had scheduled a follow-up surgery. This one required the removal of body parts I wasn't sure I had the strength to lose.

.011 | LIFE IS TOO SHORT NOT TO DO THIS

HALF-NAKED, I STAND staring at my reflection. My fingers grasp the clasps of a bloodstained bra.

Frozen by the weight of the moment, I am about to see the work of the surgeon who performed my double mastectomy. The procedure required removal of tissue armpit to armpit reaching from my clavicle to below my breasts. Friends warned me that this moment could cast a shadow on the way I saw myself.

Measuring my breaths, I count down from ten.

10 . . . 9 . . . 8 . . .

How ugly will the scars be?

7 . . . 6 . . . 5 . . .

Will I look awkward in a snug-fitting sweater?

4 . . . 3 . . . 2 . . .

Will my husband still find me attractive?

1 . . .

The bra is locked tight to stabilize everything for optimal healing. I tug back and forth to unlatch the clasps. Each pop makes me wince. The bra falls to the floor. Ever so tender, I peel away layers of gauze.

I can see it now. All of it. Every stitch and scab.

My eyes follow the interlocking roadways of tape. Four grenade-shaped drains hang, two on each side, collecting the fluid leaking from my body. The landscape is swollen and bruised. I count the number of bright red incisions, stopping when I reach double digits. A war has been fought on my body. These are my battle wounds.

I am shocked.

But not like one might expect.

I am shocked that I'm *not* shocked.

Women who had gone before me told me horror stories about this infamous surgery. The descriptions played in my mind. The gruesome scars. The absence of nipples. The permanent numbness. An array of horrific visions swoop into my mind like kamikaze pilots.

Yet somehow I'm not blown back by the mutilation.

Those scars inside my chest are far more grisly. The ruddy marks in the mirror promise to fade over time. My body will heal, the cragged lines dwindling into faint reminders and memories. I feel less certain about the invisible wounds I collected since the diagnosis.

The Queen warned us at one of the first appointments that Leif and I might encounter relational speed bumps upon sharing our situation: "As you make the news public, beware. Some of the people you expect will be there for you will vanish."

Leif and I placated her with unconvincing nods. We had walked through so much with so many already that we both felt confident our community would stand stalwart.

Within weeks, The Queen's forecast came true.

Silence.

Indifference.

Abandonment.

Announcing my diagnosis was like hanging a bug zapper on a riverboat at midnight. Friends rushed in like winged insects attracted to the strange phosphorescent glow. They overcame us with love, prayers, and support for days.

Bzzzzt!

Then, one by one, they spiraled into the darkness. Our phone stopped vibrating. Knocks at the door grew further apart until they stopped altogether.

I developed a budding friendship with Annie prior to my diagnosis. We'd even planned a fun weekend together. When adversity hit, my calendar was hijacked by medical appointments and consultations, tests and treatments. I reluctantly canceled. I never heard from her again.

Others we'd known for longer than a decade never spoke a word. Not even a "thinking of you" text message. People with whom we'd shared many meals. They had stayed in our home and were privy to secrets. Our lives had tangled like vines over the years. Their absence stung.

They knew. We knew they knew. They knew we knew they knew. Yet there was only silence.

I considered that they, perhaps, were trying to be respectful, afraid any communication would be intrusive. Had my requests to friends and family for space to work through the details and logistics been interpreted as a request for no communication at all? Could it have just been a misunderstanding? Perhaps they faced their own crisis and didn't want to burden us. Many felt helpless.

Sometimes in the darkness, I would try to imagine what others might be thinking: *What do you say to the cancer patient fighting for her life when my biggest problem is getting our daughter to call home from college?* Unsure of how to respond, they withdrew.

If they only knew.

I tried to extend the benefit of the doubt again and again. When I struggled most I reminded myself that I'd been guilty of these ill responses and more over the years.

When I had strength, I attempted to reach out. I called a childhood friend, someone I had known for more than twenty-five years, someone I grieved with after her father disappeared in a plane crash. My communication went without reply.

I followed up with a text: "Did you receive my message?"

"I have thought about you every day since and what I wanted to say," she texted back. "I am in shock, and yet I don't know how to respond. I'm scared. And I love you."

My sweet friend captured the heart of many. Not knowing what to say, they said nothing at all. I tried to empathize, but the silence still hurt.

Anyone who loves deep knows the pain of such inflictions. Wounds of the heart happen when you need the gift of someone's presence most and the person disappears, says something unintentionally hurtful, or lives so self-absorbed they barely see you at all. The absence cuts; the silence stings.

Your circle of friends sliced in half after the breakup or divorce. You felt abandoned after your spouse was fired from work. You haven't heard a word from your neighbors since the move. Your friends were nowhere to be found a few weeks after the funeral. You couldn't help but notice the row of seats left empty by those who promised they'd be there. One by one, they stopped calling, stopped e-mailing, stopped messaging.

The deepest wounds in war come from friendly fire. The people closest to us have the power to hurt us the most.

Sure, Leif and I had our team. The Queen. Our parents. Those who continued to support us through the many months with phone calls, texts, e-mails, and gifts. The initial outpouring was strong, but as time wore on, many vanished like breath in late winter.

The throbbing that screamed loudest emanated not from the jagged flesh of my chest, but from the wounds of my heart. Long after my physical marks faded, these deeper ones would remain sensitive to the touch.

Standing before the mirror, I remember that the sharp tip of a surgeon's knife can never cut as deeply as those we love.

I know how you feel.

That's what I think Jesus would say had he been standing in front of the mirror with me. Though he warned the disciples that his earthly ministry would come to an abrupt, brutal end, they didn't understand.

Who can blame them?

I imagine the disciples camping under many a starry night, reflecting on the day's unforgettable events. Hiking hundreds of miles of dusty roads, the hand-plucked twelve dream about what the future holds for them. Sailing the sea, they wonder what miracles Jesus might perform when they land ashore.

Day after day, they witness the impossible unfold.

A withered hand sprouts fingers. Cloudy eyes clear to perfect vision. Corpses breathe life, crippled feet dance, even madmen regain sanity. The disciples wait for Jesus to take his position on Israel's throne.

Gathered around the table before Passover, Jesus continues to astound the disciples. On an evening he would have been justified to throw in the towel, Jesus picks one up instead. He washes the toes of everyone in the room. Together, they crunch on charred bread and sip wine. Jesus' eyes scan the room before resting on the cup before him. The color drains from his weathered brown cheeks. His jaw tightens, then releases. With pained reluctance, Jesus delivers difficult news to the disciples: a betrayer sits among them.

The disciples' foreheads crinkle as a cloud of anguish and disbelief descends. Jesus' sayings are often difficult to swallow—who could forget that whole "love your enemy" message?—but this one lodges in their throats.

I knew Bartholomew wasn't to be trusted, Philip thinks. *That guy has barely said a word since we picked him up.*

Andrew eyeballs James, Simon casts a disapproving glance at Matthew, and Thomas starts doubting that any of this is really happening.

The faces are familiar. No stranger slipped in unnoticed. So which one of them could it be? This is a gathering of the tried-and-true. Who on earth could Jesus be referring to?

Peter nudges the disciple whom Jesus loves to press for more details.

"Lord, who is it?" the disciple asks.

Jesus refuses to speak the perpetrator's name, but he exposes the betrayer with a cryptic response: "It is the one to whom I will give this piece of bread when I have dipped it in the dish."

A soppy chunk of crust emerges from the cup then presses into Judas's palm with the instruction: do it fast.

Whenever the tale is retold today, we have the advantage of knowing how the story ends. Like watching a whodunit movie a second time, the sleight of hand and trickery becomes impossible to miss. We're clicking our tongues at Judas before the bread breaks the wine's surface.

Imagining Judas as a shifty-eyed shyster lurking in the shadows is natural. We may assume that, in order to follow Jesus, Judas left his dilapidated house on Shady Lane. Nothing could be further from the truth.

Judas moves among Jesus' inner circle, one of the most trusted of the Twelve. He takes responsibility for the money. Judas is the CFO, the chairman of the stewardship committee. He keeps the disciples fed and manages caring for the poor.

Judas enjoys orchestra seats to Jesus' greatest miracles and most powerful teachings. On many a night, along with the other disciples, he gathers around the campfire and laughs until his belly aches.

No wonder the disciples are befuddled by the exchange. The Gospel of John emphasizes the lack of comprehension by highlighting it twice. Among the remaining disciples, "no one at the meal understood" and they "stared at one another, at a loss." Those who had logged countless miles with Jesus now gape in silence, unable to comprehend what has transpired.

Judas is Jesus' buddy. His companion. His confidant.

Besides, what kind of person bathes and feeds someone about to stab him in the back? Would you? Would I?

Worse, Judas isn't the lone betrayer in Jesus' address book. The evening begins with a dozen disciples, but only one remains at the foot of the cross the next day. Where did Jesus' friends go? Peter declares himself ready to die for Christ but in a twenty-four-hour span offers an unholy trinity of denials. Everyone else runs for the hills like their hair is on fire. The disciples who promised to stand by their rabbi crawl into closets and hide behind dumpsters. So much for friendship.

The betrayal of the Son of God extends further. Jesus stands before a crowd, many squatting at his feet, witnessing his healings firsthand. Days before, they cheered his arrival into Jerusalem and waved palm branches in exuberance.

Surely they will remain by their Savior, the long-awaited Messiah. Alas, they end up liberating an insurrectionist, Barabbas, and sending Jesus away with a death sentence. How fickle and cruel.

The road to resurrection is paved with disloyalty, buffered by guardrails of isolation, marked with the skid marks of failing friendships.

Though no one has walked quite the same path or even approached the anguish Jesus experienced, it's easy to empathize. Most of us have felt the sting of betrayal or the ache of abandonment:

The family member who stole your innocence as a child.

The jilt of a spouse who confessed to having an affair.

The employee who cozied up to you then pilfered your accounts.

The confidant who shared your deepest secrets with others.

The friends who disappeared when you needed them most.

Betrayal is one of the most painful acts we can inflict on another human. Even Dante made it the ninth circle of hell in his *Inferno*. Such relational duplicity may not leave the visible scars of a knife or scalpel, but still cuts to the core. We are created for communion with God and one another; abandonment is fundamentally wounding. Betrayal slices through our ability to trust and punctures our willingness to risk vulnerability.

The only thing more startling than the extent to which Jesus is betrayed is his response. He continues to love, serve, and give to his friends—*all* his friends—even to the bitter end.

This loving-kindness spills to the crowds that convict him. Though the masses transform into a mob, Jesus offers his life that they might be reconciled to God. Jesus bets on those who roll dice for his clothes, extends grace to those who hurl insults, and speaks in defense of those who watch in silence: "Father, forgive them, for they know not what they do."

Such sturdy resolve overflows to the disciples after the resurrection. Instead of recoiling, Jesus reaches out to his deserters—appearing to the disciples again and again, affirming them in love. As for poor Peter, weighed down by an extra helping of guilt and shame, Jesus seems to hug him extra tight.

Jesus pours out his blood on the heads and heels of his traitors. He gives himself for the takers, offers presence to those absent, and dies for those who flee for their lives.

In life's most significant moments, our minds become cameras. Every blink captures images of those who cheer when we grasp the diploma, toss rice at the wedding, weep at the funeral. We catalog those present and collect snapshots of those absent too.

Standing in front of the mirror, I saw the images of those I counted as betrayers and deniers. I winced as I recalled the names of the members of my inner circle who rushed away at the first sign of trouble. The memories stabbed my soul. Now I was the table host, and I didn't know if I had the strength to feed, water, or wash their feet.

Jesus, I want healing for my heart scars. Help me forgive.

Pulling out a blank sheet of paper, I repeated the question: "Who, Holy Spirit, who?"

Names flooded my mind. I scrawled them down and made note of what the person had done or left undone that resulted in the hurt, disappointment, or a sense of betrayal. Names flowed fast and then slowed to a drip before running dry.

My chicken scratch revealed an unexpected pattern—the greatest feeling of betrayal came from those who vanished, those who said nothing, those whose response could be summed up in a single word: silence. Abandonment is its own form of betrayal.

But some who stay also wreak havoc.

They fall into four categories. *Projectors* attempt to turn every crisis into their crisis so they don't have to face their own issues. *Pretenders* seem more interested in landing the latest scoop than caring for those in need. *Predators* like to harvest others' hardship for their gain. *Pain inflictors* break the silence in a hurtful or unhelpful way with cruel or cold comments.

Peppered in the list were acquaintances I had encountered along the way. The nurse who forgot a much-needed shot, leaving me with a compromised immune system and forcing me into quarantine. The doctor who told me to "pull it together" after we'd received devastating news. The personnel in hospital billing, those who worked the call center at the insurance company, and that lab that mischarged us five months in a row.

Every name represented a gash in my heart. Every name represented an opportunity to experience the joy and freedom that comes with forgiveness.

"I forgive," I said aloud, offering clemency to each person for what they had done or left undone.

God, you know how they hurt me. Help me forgive.

Then I considered what it meant to love these until the bitter end. What would my towel and basin look like?

I offered a blessing over each name.

Father, I ask that you demonstrate your favor, and comfort this person with your grace.

Halfway down the list, spontaneous acts of kindness came to mind.

I phoned several friends and apologized that we hadn't connected in a while. I invited others to dinner. I took several to lunch, making sure to pick up the check. For some, the best response was to drop a handwritten note that I was thinking of and praying for them.

Somewhere along the way I stumbled on the joy that comes with making mangled relationships whole. It didn't follow every conversation or meal, but some of the relationships flourished with renewed energy. Others just felt at peace again.

Then there was Annie. What could I do for her to bring healing? I decided to send her a box of pears and thank her for the budding friendship we'd cultivated. The friendship had ended abruptly but bore fruit prior. The present seemed fitting.

Jesus' life demonstrates the importance of loving, serving, and giving ourselves to those who betray and abandon us. That doesn't mean we become a doormat or that some friendships don't cross the threshold of a necessary ending. We can choose to trade the pangs of bitterness for the expansive joy that comes with forgiveness.

I continued to add names as they entered my mind over the following days. Reading through the list made me wonder about all those I had betrayed. The ones I had forgotten while focusing on my own pain. Forgiveness is a busy highway, not just a one-way street.

Flipping over the paper, I scribbled another list of names. Beth, with the difficult pregnancy. Ryan, who learned he had multiple sclerosis. Mark and Rebecca, who struggled to parent their autistic child. Sally, whose husband announced he was gay after nineteen years of marriage. Friends who had been laid off. The missionaries in Africa whose nation erupted in violence.

It was my turn to pick up the phone, say "I'm sorry," and serve them.

More healing set in with each call and note as if I were unwrapping the bandages of my heart and allowing the scars to breathe. Like the bright wounds across my chest, the internal ones were beginning to mend.

Something was missing. I had forgiven some and apologized to others. Still some of the most important names were missing—those I needed to give two simple but potent words: "Thank you!"

These names flowed faster than any others.

Janella had allowed me to boo-hoo on my most grief-filled days. Peggy and Louie had mailed cards every month for a year. Tyler broke the silence by calling to apologize for his disappearance. That conversation solidified our friendship and taught me that one call *really* can make all the difference.

The lists that had been a place of pain became a portal for healing. That's when I discovered:

**Joy expands with every
"I forgive," "I'm sorry," and "thank you."**

After all, that's what our heavenly Father has done for us.

He healed humanity by breaking the silence. God sent Jesus, the Word, to be with us. That's why we can give the gift of presence, because we've received God's presence.

Rather than look to others, we can be the ones who break the silence. The ones who find joy in becoming ambassadors of reconciliation. The ones who offer the gift of our presence no matter how difficult the situation.

What lists do you need to make? Who do you need to forgive? Where do you need to interrupt the silence and say, "I'm sorry"? What can you do to begin the process of reconciliation, not with backhanded slight but a genuine expression of friendship? Like Christ, how can you love to the bitter end?

It's never too late.

I was learning the oil of forgiveness could help heal many a battle scar. But perhaps the most profound lesson I received was from a friend who never walked away.

.012 | WHERE I NEVER EXPECTED TO FIND JOY

WHEN I EMBARKED on this joy expedition, I had no idea I'd be plunged into a sea of helplessness and pain, depression and disease. Even though a cancer diagnosis is shipwrecking, we are all swimming through the muck called life.

At the end of my radiation treatments, I decided to take stock. I had physically survived. I was still breathing. My life had been spared, at least for now.

So why did I feel sad? Why did I feel like I was still in mourning? Shouldn't I be living in unspeakable, uncontainable, uncontrollable joy? Isn't this what we prayed for?

As I surveyed our situation, I realized our lives hadn't just changed. Our home had too.

Several months into chemotherapy, I tired of the fleshy peach walls of our house. My decorator friend, Laura, advised us on a new palette. She helped us select fresh colors, and before long, the walls took on a tone of deep slate.

Maybe this dark grey reflected my desire not to limit my accent color options. Or perhaps it mirrored the shade of my spirit these many months. Most days, I was neither up nor down, gloomy nor elated, hopeless nor certain that tomorrow would be better. Which is to say, I spent most days like you may: in the tension of in-between emotions.

After learning to fight every circumstance with joy, I decided to create space for the virtue throughout our home.

"We want to create a joy wall," I told Laura as we discussed what to hang atop the fresh paint.

Laura first inspired the idea when we went to Denver's Paris Street Market the previous spring, a monthly shopping event consisting of a parking lot full of clothes, jewelry, shabby chic furniture, and whatnot. We walked booth to booth, admiring the oddities—chandeliers fashioned from mason jars, tree-trunk tables with barrels for seating, and an old dresser painted with a chevron pattern, refitted with ivory hardware.

We approached a tent with metal consonants and vowels strewn across the ground in colors ranging from canary yellow to jet-black. Some had been nibbled on by rust, others punctured by drill holes and bullets. A handful boasted light bulbs.

"I have it right here," a sugary Southern voice announced from the back of the makeshift booth.

Laura eagerly grabbed a two-foot-tall pink metal *p* from the saleswoman's hands. She thrust a wad of cash into the woman's hand and cradled the *p* tightly under her arm.

"What are you spelling?" I asked.

"A three-word declaration for our living room," she said.

"What is it?" I pressed.

"Happy Are We." she said, pausing between each word. "I've been collecting them for years, and this is the final letter! When I started, I came across this big, beautiful *y*. The letter was so spectacular I just had to buy it first."

That evening I couldn't get those big ol' rusty metal letters out of my mind. I kept thinking about the way Laura had constructed a daring declaration in the middle of her home as a constant reminder of her heart's desire. *What if I did the same?*

Leif and I had made plenty of declarations in our lives—usually with our choices rather than our lips:

Busy Are We.

Tired Are We.

Striving Are We.

Anxious Are We.

Frustrated Are We.

Stuck Are We.

Discontent Are We.

Restless Are We.

Jealous Are We.

Discouraged Are We.

Angry Are We.

Cynical Are We.

Ungrateful Are We.

The thought of someone walking into our house and stumbling on one of these statements tucked into a cluttered corner, let alone displayed in bold letters on our living room wall, made me cringe.

Recalibrating, I imagined the blank wall filled from floor to ceiling with a kaleidoscope of colorful expressions:

Loving Are We.

Pee-Your-Pants-Good-Time Are We.

Peaceful Are We.

Patient Are We

Kind Are We.

Good-Hearted Are We.

Faithful Are We.

Gentle Are We.

Self-Controlled Are We.

Thankful Are We.

Content Are We.

Blessed Are We.

Those were all viable options, but another phrase lingered that seemed more aligned with my heart:

Joyful are we!

More than anything, I wanted that to become the center-piece of my life.

When I explained the idea to Laura, she challenged us to look for items, even in our painful journey, that represented joy to us. Leif and I scrambled through the house unearthing meaningful treasures. A framed piece of artwork stashed under the bed. Photos crammed in a desk drawer. A plastic bag jammed with notes from those who had been praying for us.

Laura laid the items on the living room floor. The collection looked like leftovers from a country church rummage sale. With the eye of a designer, she aligned them according to color and size and texture.

In a downtown market, Leif and I found frames to spray-paint, mason jars to hold all those meaningful cards, and knickknacks that represented joy to us.

By the time the joy wall was finished, we all stood back in awe. Every detail served as a living reminder of God's goodness and grace.

Along one side, we placed a spider web from the museum in Vermont. Beside it hung images of snowflakes from the Snowflake Bentley Museum. Below that, a photo of those who survived the botched hike in Maine. A small wooden peg protruded from the wall. On it rested a hat whose tag read *Grace.*

In the corner of the room, a stray red balloon floated in the air. Just one more memento I'd been keeping in my home reminding me to never stop fighting back with joy.

This journey helped me discover that happiness isn't spelled the way we thought. Neither is joy.

Joy flows out of unsuspecting, and often daunting, places. It's illogical, irrational, downright crazypants to think that great adversity could possibly lead to a fuller life. Yet that's what I've discovered over many months of being poisoned, burned, injected, sliced, and diced.

I never imagined I'd find joy in waiting rooms, MRI machines, wig shops, and hiking trails. I didn't know that joy could be mixed into cookie batter or heard in the ripping of a blouse. That it could fall with tears and rise with balloons.

The landscape of my life looks much different now. Joy is the weaponry I've used to fight back disease, disillusionment, depression.

Make no mistake: I do not count cancer a gift. As I squint through the darkness of these events, I have discovered gifts along the way. Friendships have been fortified. My relationship with Leif brims with a tenderness and affection that we never knew before. My spiritual life has been enriched by moments when God broke the silence in the midst of great affliction.

In the wake of my dad's cancer diagnosis, I heard him say "I love you" more than ever before. As I write this, we just learned that the treatment for him worked too. Yet another reason to pull out the party hats and celebrate.

Though I don't wish adversity on anyone, the suffering has cracked open my heart to more pain and also more joy than I knew possible. The many tears drilled deep wells of compassion. I've even begun to embrace unknowing.

I've learned to practice a defiant joy—one that is my heritage, my purpose, and my destiny—and in the process my life is marked by more gratitude than ever.

That said, some mornings, crawling out of bed is a major accomplishment. A day without pain, a triumph. A drive to the hospital without breathing into a paper bag, a victory.

Hardships have a way of making us wonder if God has gone silent or abandoned us. We may be tempted to misinterpret circumstances as a sign of God shoving us away or strain to understand why God didn't intervene to stop the calamity. We may feel alone.

But we're not.

I'm lying in bed now in a torrent of familiar tears. I miss the former life, the former body, the former Margaret so much. I long for her energy and liveliness and Tigger-like bounce, the unmutilated body, the unblurred mind, the effortless creativity, the strength that always renewed.

"You must not have liked her very much," I say to God, teary pools collecting above my cheeks.

Quite the contrary, he answers. *I loved her so much that even in this I want her to look more like my Son.*

In the cool darkness of the bedroom, the sense of God's fierce love rises within me and with it glimmers of joy. I peel back the covers and tiptoe into the living room. The moonlight seeps through the windows, washing my joy wall with light. My fingertips brush across the letters and pictures from this winding road. Reminders of God's providence these many months, and also of his grace.

Standing in front of the hodgepodge wall, I realize that fighting with joy is without beginning or end. This year, the fight is cancer. Next year, it may be financial struggle. A decade from now, it may be the snares of midlife existence. After that, it may be wrestling with the death of loved ones. The wall before me is not just a series of reminders about what I have been through; it is a collection of tools for the fights that yet lie ahead. I can hear the cannon fire in the distance from battles I may be able to delay but cannot avoid.

The salty tears have made their way to the corners of my mouth now, but I can also taste resolve.

I have only begun to fight back with joy.

5 Things to Say When You Don't Know What to Say

SOMEONE YOU KNOW receives dreaded news. A diagnosis. A divorce. Unemployment. A major loss.

You may feel ill-prepared and unequipped to enter into someone's crisis. You don't know the person that well. You count the months and years since you lost touch, and it feels strange, even foreign, to reach out now. You may even second-guess if contacting the person is appropriate. What will the person or their family think?

The reasons to remain silent pile high until you reach the ultimate: "I don't know what to say." Saying nothing seems better than saying the wrong thing. Or is it?

Your presence is one of the most meaningful, powerful things to offer to someone suffering hardship. How do you break the silence in a way that brings life and hope and encouragement?

In the case of the loss of a loved one, it's appropriate to say something about your own sorrow at learning of the person's death and something specific you will miss about the person.

For most other losses and crises, this is not a time to tell your story, compare your experiences, process your grief, or share what you've learned through crisis. All the attention and compassion should be on the other person. Avoid making assumptions about what the person is feeling, thinking, experiencing, or needing since no two crises or grief experiences are the same.

Keep your words few. Remember Job's friends, who circled around him after his earth-shattering crisis. For seven days, they were a balm and blessing. Then they got into trouble when they opened their mouths. We do too.

Here are five things to say to break the silence and still bring healing to those experiencing crisis:

1. "Know that you are loved and prayed for today."

These words express remembrance, compassion, and the gift of presence. They make those of us who suffer the central concern. These words penetrate absence and subtly encourage us that we aren't alone. God is with us too.

2. "My heart aches with you and for you today."

These words acknowledge that you feel the pangs of grief but still center on the those of us who are hurting. This makes us the focus of concern and compassion while acknowledging that you are with us and for us.

3. "I have experienced loss, and I am so sorry for what you're going through."

If you have experienced similar grief, this opens the possibility of "comforting those with the comfort you've received" (2 Corinthians 1:4). We may not be in the mood to chitchat or may find great comfort in connecting with you. If we ask you to share, remember to maintain the focus on our current loss and grief even as you share from your own. This can be a gift to those of us feeling alone, isolated, or unsure about what we're feeling or thinking.

4. "If you have a specific prayer request, I'd be honored to pray for you. But in the meantime, know that I'm praying for you and asking God how to pray for you best."

When a crisis hits, many people want to know how they can pray. This well-meaning question can become tiring to those facing great loss or pain. Specific prayer requests can be hard to identify, can change every day, or may not be public information. Remember you don't need specific details to pray for us. Break the silence by letting us know you're committed to pray for us, with or without details, and continually petitioning God on our behalf.

5. "You are so loved! What specific thing can I do and/or provide that would help you right now? Let me know— and if you don't have any ideas, I have suggestions."

Many people think they know what someone needs without asking the person. The result is often an abundance of one or two resources and a lack of other needs being met. The refrigerator fills with casseroles that soon go bad; the closets overflow with blankets while medical bills go unpaid and the lawn isn't mowed for months.

Always ask what someone needs. Come prepared with practical ideas, because we may not be able to identify our needs or needs may change on a day-to-day basis. Offer a gift card to a gas station, pharmacy, or grocery store. Suggest prepaying for several hours of handyman or cleaning service. Offer an afternoon watching a comedy to get out of the house and laugh. If you have access, suggest a weekend getaway at your family's cabin. Provide an evening of childcare. Remember the needs of the spouse and kids too.

Even your most humble offerings of presence and sincere care can make a huge difference.

For more ideas on how to serve those in crisis, visit
www.margaretfeinberg.com/fightbackwithjoy

8 Things Those Facing Crisis Can't Tell You (But Wish They Could)

WE WERE NOT CREATED for death or grief or disease or disaster. Perhaps that's why it's so hard to know how to respond. We don't know what to say. We can't imagine what the other person is thinking or going through. Our feelings aren't their feelings. Our projected needs aren't their actual needs. Here are some things those facing crisis can't tell you but wish they could.

1. "Reach out to me."
We need you to break the silence. Many people are looky-loos—the kind of people who slow down at the scene of an accident. They read the details of the crash and share them with their coworkers and friends, but never reach out to the victim directly. They may get updates from other people, but they never interact with us.

That's why we need you to reach out and break the silence. No matter how much time has gone by. Your presence matters. When you reach out it means more to us than you'll never know.

2. "Notice me."

The desire to try to connect with a person's loss is strong, but sometimes it can take the conversation to unhealthy places. This is not the time to process your pain. Simply listen without trying to fix the situation or us. We just need you to be with us and for us. Notice us and pay attention to our needs. Some days we need to commiserate; other days we need you to distract us with fun stories. When you're unsure of our needs, ask, "What do you need from me right now?"

3. "Do what you say you're going to do."

We need you to do what you say you're going to do. Don't promise to loan yard equipment, provide lunch, or help tackle a project around the house and not follow through. Don't say, "I'll do anything" to those in crisis. Instead, let us know you want to help, and make specific suggestions of needs you can realistically meet.

4. "Ask God how to pray for me."

Praying for us is good, but asking God how to pray is better. Lots of people say they'll pray for us, but some days it's just hard to believe. Ask if you can pray with us. Be ready (and not offended) if we say no. When we say yes, instead of praying for what you think we need, ask the Holy Spirit how to pray before you begin.

5. "Don't give me any clichés."

Skip the Bible clichés. This is not the time to remind us that God has a plan or God works all things for good or God is going use this to fill-in-the-blank. Avoid mentioning anything about God's will. Such words can bruise rather than bless, hurt rather than heal. If you share a Bible passage, make sure it's been meaningful to you in your own time of suffering. Pray about when and how to share the scripture. Always do so with gentleness and grace.

6. "Meet my real needs."

Many of us who have gone through a crisis end up with mountains of well-meaning but unhelpful clutter. After the thank-you cards are written, many of the items are donated to charity, tossed in the trash, or worse, become a burden for those of us who grapple with, "What do I do with this now?" and "Do I have to keep this?" Instead of filling a person's life with trinkets, ask what the person needs. The person may need help paying legal or medical bills, buying groceries, making a mortgage or rent payment, or caring for their children.

7. "Remember my family."

Caregivers and kids get tired too. Shower attention on them. When you visit, pop by to tell them hello. Ask what they need. Give a massage gift certificate to the caregiver or throw a pizza night for the children. Let them know you're praying for them too. If you know the family well, spend one-on-one time with the kids and listen to them, even if they say or do something outrageous. They are also processing grief and may need a safe place to express anger, sadness, and ask tough questions.

8. "Stay with me."

Ambulance chasers are a dime a dozen; rebuilders are hard to find. Swarms of people appear on the scene of a crisis, but six months later they're nowhere to be found. Crisis doesn't end when the funeral is over, radiation ends, divorce papers are filed, or the lawsuit is finalized. It continues for months and even years afterward. If you have a meaningful friendship with someone who has experienced great loss, consider setting a reminder on your calendar to check back every few weeks. Keep letting them know that you love them, you're praying for them, and you're still with them.

Join the conversation online. What has been most
helpful and meaningful to you during a time of crisis?
Post your response at
www.margaretfeinberg.com/fightbackwithjoy
or use #fightbackwithjoy
on Instagram, Twitter, Facebook, or Pinterest.

6 Lessons I Learned from Crisis

IF YOU'RE ENTERING the battlefield and choosing to fight back with joy, you're not alone. If I could meet you in person, I'd give you a hug, a red balloon, and ask to hear your story. And if you asked what I've learned during my own crisis this past year, here are some lessons I'd share.

1. Crisis changes our lives.

All of us experience loss. The loss may arrive through a single event or series of them. Sometimes the loss is public, a devastation that can't be hidden as hard as we try. Other times it's private; few souls know. These encounters with crisis are refining moments in our lives. Life will never go back exactly to what it was. We are different now. We must learn to live a new normal.

2. Crisis changes us.

Most people who have experienced trauma feel like they've lost a part of themselves. Loss rebrands our identities. Sometimes the new labels thrust on us feel foreign. Words like *divorcée, widow, single parent, cancer patient, autistic, orphan,* or *convict* challenge our identities. As we come to the end of ourselves, we open the door to discovering the One who created us anew. The One who can whisper to us who we really are as we pilgrim toward our truest and deepest selves.

3. Healing takes much time.

When we experience significant loss, it's normal to ache for our old lives. Healing of our minds, hearts, emotions, and bodies takes time; the path to wholeness is anything but straight. The terrain is steep, the path winding curlicues. The anniversary of the loss can make us wonder if we've made any progress at all. Healing takes a long time. We must learn to be patient with others and ourselves as we courageously take this journey.

4. Mixed emotions are normal.

Loss, crisis, and trauma expand our emotional bandwidth. Feelings that once seemed opposites now intertwine. We erupt in laughter as tears flow. Hope and despair cross paths in our hearts. The coolness of peace intersects with hot anger. Rather than suppress our emotions, we need to recognize them as healing our souls. Don't be afraid to feel. Be afraid when you stop feeling.

5. No two traumas are equal.

Our culture likes to rank and quantify loss. How many people died? How many cars were involved in the pileup? How much will the rebuild cost after the natural disaster? Though news reporters tally losses, we must not. No two losses are ever the same. Even if they share the same diagnosis, description, or name, every loss inflicts a different kind pain on the person enduring it. We must resist the temptation to compare and quantify losses.

6. Running from sorrow will only take you to scary places.

Running from sorrow never leads anywhere good. Moments of pleasure that provide windows of escape soon become sources of temptation. Perhaps this is why many who go through trauma become addicts. Food. Alcohol. Sex. Prescription drugs. Shopping. Work. Gaming. Television. We must face sorrow with courage. Learn to grieve in a healthy way. If needed, seek the help of a professional counselor to embrace sorrow in a way that leads to healing and restoration.

A Letter from Leif

Dear Friend,

Having wrestled adversity by Margaret's side, I can tell you caring for an ailing loved one is one of life's great challenges. Caregiving isn't easy at the best of times. Watching the person I love suffer and in pain made me feel helpless and frustrated on multiple levels (at myself, at her, and at God for allowing the situation). When you are in a battle like I've faced, I hope a little of what I've learned might help.

1. Take time for yourself without feeling guilty.

You can't be a good caregiver if you aren't taking care of yourself. Much of your time, energy, and schedule revolves around their needs. When possible and appropriate, arrange for a trusted person to stay with your loved one while you take a time-out for yourself, away from the house or hospital. Do something that refreshes or invigorates you. On especially difficult days, I would release anger and recharge by playing thirty minutes of video games and or exercising with my swim team. That worked for me, but do what works for you.

2. Form your own team.

Caregivers also experience grief, loss, and trauma. Our grief may be different, but we still need support. Meet with a trusted friend or Christian counselor to wrestle through fears, grief, and emotions. I selected friends who had experienced similar situations and would allow me to vent. I reached out to them for feedback, prayer, and whenever I needed a sounding board. Don't bottle stuff up—it always comes out—and know what you are feeling is valid. Encourage your support system to reach out to you when you may not feel up to reaching out to them.

3. Know your limits.

Be realistic about your time and energy levels. Caregiving diminishes your emotional and physical bandwidth. Recognize that some nights dinner will come from the deli counter or a bag of microwave popcorn. Plan ahead for doctor's appointments. Consider asking a friend or family member to prepare a meal for you when you get home. Set boundaries in terms of amounts and types of food (allergies or preferences) and dropping off versus staying to share the meal together. Such details are critical to communicate to those who want to be helpful rather than making the situation more difficult.

4. Express your emotions in front of your loved one.

You may be tempted to put on a brave face for your loved one, but finding the right place, time, and way to express your grief, angst, frustration, and fear allows your loved one the freedom to be honest with you too. This is critical if you want to maintain a healthy relationship. If Margaret and I hadn't worked at this, making a lot of mistakes along the way, I might have started to see Margaret as a person with problems to fix rather than as my spouse. This may not be fitting for your situation, but do your best to communicate with your loved one when appropriate.

5. Don't forget to celebrate.

As part of fighting back with joy, Margaret and I made every victory—no matter how small—a chance to celebrate. Savoring dinner at our favorite restaurant. Holding hands as we walked out of the hospital. Sharing a funny e-mail, article, or picture that made us laugh. Planning future trips or parties. Studies show that more than half the enjoyment is in the anticipation of an event. We celebrated the planning of various trips, excursions, and meals.

My hope and prayer is that you will find God sustaining you every step of the way and that you, too, will choose to fight back with joy.

In His grip and for His glory,
Leif

Playlist

MUSIC AWAKENS THE heart. This is a list of suggested songs to accompany your journey through the chapters of *Fight Back With Joy*. If you find other songs that are great fits, please let me know at joy@margaretfeinberg.com.

.000 | Why We Live Joyless Lives
"Wake Me Up," Avicii, *True*
"Oceans (Where Feet May Fail)," Hillsong United, *Zion*
"Manifesto," The City Harmonic, *I Have a Dream (It Feels Like Home)*

.001 | A Choice That Changed Everything
"Multiplied," NEEDTOBREATHE, *Rivers in the Wasteland*
"Brave," Sara Bareilles, *The Blessed Unrest*
"Joy," The Rend Collective, *The Art of Celebration*

.002 | The Living, Breathing Gift of Joy
"I'll Fight," Daughtry, *Baptized*
"Ordinary Love," U2, *Mandela: Long Walk to Freedom (Original Motion Picture Soundtrack)*
"God Gave Me You," Dave Barnes, *What We Want, What We Get*

.003 | Three Simple Words to Set You Free

"Roll Away Your Stone," Mumford & Sons, *The Road to Red Rocks (Live)*

"Let It Go," Idina Menzel, *Frozen*

"We Are Blessed," All Sons and Daughters, *The Longing EP*

.004 | The Biggest Myth about Joy

"Fireflies," Owl City, *Ocean Eyes*

"Diamonds," Johnnyswim, *Diamonds*

"You Make Me Brave," Bethel Music, *You Make Me Brave*

.005 | When You're Tearing Your Hair Out

"I Am Not Alone," Kari Jobe, *Majestic (Live)*

"I Am," Crowder, *Neon Steeple*

"Hold Me Jesus," Rich Mullins, *A Liturgy, A Legacy & A Ragamuffin Band*

.006 | How to Throw the Best Party Ever

"Life in Color," OneRepublic, *Native*

"Roar," Katy Perry, *PRISM*

"Best Day of My Life," American Authors, *Oh, What a Life*

.007 | The Side of Joy No One Talks About

"Broken Hallelujah," The Afters, *Life Is Beautiful*

"10,000 Reasons (Bless the Lord)," Matt Redman, *10,000 Reasons*

"Beautiful Lord," Leeland, *Sound of Melodies*

.008 | One Prayer You Don't Pray But Should

"From This Valley," The Civil Wars, *Bare Bones EP*

"Heart Beats," Johnnyswim, *Home*
"Home," Phillip Phillips, *The World from the Side of the Moon*

.009 | You've Got to Give This Away
"Make You Feel My Love," Adele, *19*
"Let Them See You," JJ Weeks Band, *All Over the World*
"I Refuse," Josh Wilson, *See You*

.010 | When Nothing Means Everything
"Even If (The Healing Doesn't Come)," Kutless, *Apologies*
"Worn," Tenth Avenue North, *The Struggle*
"It Is Well with My Soul," Jeremy Camp, *How Great Thou Art: Timeless Hymns—Modern Voices*

.011 | Life Is Too Short Not to Do This
"Invisible," U2, *(RED) Edit Version*
"Changed," Rascal Flatts, *Changed*
"Back to December," Taylor Swift, *Speak Now*

.012 | Where I Never Expected to Find Joy
"Overcomer," Mandisa, *Overcomer*
"Happy," Pharrell Williams, *Despicable Me 2 (Original Motion Picture Soundtrack)*
"This Is the Day," Phil Wickham, *Response*

Abundant Thanks

To LEIF, who continues to embody the love of God to me every day. I'm the luckiest woman on the planet. Thank you for picking me.

To Mom and Dad, for loving and praying me through the house of horrors.

To Jonathan Merritt, who wrote when I could only weep and turned my mourning into joy. Without you, this book would not be possible.

To Cammy and Jerry Johnson, Coke, Gary, Marj, Hans, Susan, Jens, Cleve, Psalm, Klyr, and Noe Oines, and Doug and Melodee Anderson for all your prayers and love.

To Carol Rykiel, Amy O'Donnell, Dave Terpstra, K. B. Hom, Debra Anderson, Joel, Emily, and Jana Malm, Nancy Franson, Kathy Lawless, Sheila Cowell, Susan St. Onge, Circe Torruellas, Patricia Barnes, Tom and Tara Lantieri, Donna Johnson, and Cherie Lowe, who helped keep me walking every day even when I was tempted to retreat into bed. To Mike and Nan James for mowing the grass and to Marty Rykiel for helping with repairs around the house. To Kara Harrison for going with us on our first visit with The Queen. To Troy and Suzanne Champ and the community of Capital Church who continue to cheer us on, and to Shelley Fliflet for praying then praying some more. To Susan Stanford for all those lovely texts.

To Jessica Johnson, who held everything together with grace and joy. You went above and beyond and were lovely every step of the way. Thank you. To Carrie Lowrie, for all your hard work, grace, and love.

To Janella Griggs, who let me say the unspeakable aloud and loved me through it all. Thank you for embodying joy and being so stinkin' funny. To Carolyn Haggard, who listened and made me laugh. You are the best kind of medicine for my soul.

To Angela Scheff, for sticking with me through this project. Editors like you only come along once in a lifetime. To Chris and Christy Ferebee, for continuing to call and extend the gift of presence.

To Ron and Susan Pinkston, Christian and Bridget Summers, Mike and Mary Sares, Frank and Naomi Overton for your friendship, love, and support. To Peggy and Louie Locke, for your love and support for so many months. You are extraordinary. To Kendall Parkhurst for dressing me with joy inside and out.

To Tracee Hackel for friendship, laugh-filled e-mails, and manuscript suggestions. To Matthew Paul Turner, Heather Zempel, Maegan Hawley, Margot Starbuck, Craig Blomberg, Byron Borger, Heather Blewett, Emily Hendrickson, Jeana Ledbetter, Janell Anema, Tyler Wigg-Stevenson, Jo Davidson, Patton Dodd, and Cathleen Falsani for kindness, encouragement, and sanding off the rougher edges.

To Taylor and Rebecca Brust, whose generosity was appreciated (and needed).

To Tom Luchin. You went above and beyond time and time again to help us through.

To Ted Cunningham. The kindness you showed us long before the diagnosis helped carry us through this difficult season.

To Hershey. I know you can't read this, but you were a trooper through all of this. Sorry for not being able to walk you for so long. Thanks for cuddling and being excited to see me on my worst days.

To our medical team. Long live The Queen!

To the Master's Swimteam at The Ridge in Littleton, Colorado, who baptized us in love and generosity. Thank you for cheering us on in generous and tangible ways. To Darren Carlile and the entire dental staff, who rallied around us with love and support. To Jeremy Williams, whose generosity was an answer to prayer.

To the team at Worthy Publishing. Thank you for being so patient and gracious on the late manuscript. I promise to turn in my doctor's note soon.

To Ray Johnson and Bayside Church, whose gift will never be forgotten. You're the only ones who have ever paid me not to speak and stay home and rest. To Kay Warren, who didn't need to reach out. You didn't have time. You did it anyway. Thank you.

To Delta Airlines, who showed us abundant grace and mercy during this challenging time. We have stood by you for years, and when we needed you, you stood by us. To the writers and actors on *Parenthood* season four, your raw storytelling was a gift that helped me catch my breath.

To I Like Giving, who helped us clear our head in the wake of the news. Thanks to Brad Forsma, for your gift and advice.

Thank you for all the kindness and prayers from Mike Stonbraker, Jean and Marc Oplinger, Lauri, Barb, and Sara Bradt, Nesha Vest, Laura Swarny, Tracey Sachman, Gerri Turner, the Catalyst Family, Dan Kimball, Kent Annan and Haiti Partners, James and Teresa Merritt, Charlie Peacock, Rich Van Pelt, Tina Lowry, Terri Spratte,

Sherry Martin, Jill Callaghan, Rob and Leah Harter, Alison Hector, Jessie Koch, Andy and Marcia Butcher, Sarah Bowling, The Taylor Family, Matt and Kori Hockett, Gary and Tammy Dunahoo, Laurie Roe, Judy Higginbotham, Rachel Mavis, Donna Kyle, Robin Carlile and Cheryl Hammet, Connie McIntyre, Alisa Laska, Barb Harris, Mary Watkins, Mike Tinnon, Kristy Hatsfelt, Marsha Young, Kristianne Stewart, Laura Schneckers, Sheila and Tony Frost, Cindy Topping, Rob and Ashley Eager, Tim and Julie Clinton, the eWomen Team and AACC, Becka and Paul Burke, The Kinnaman Family, Jerald Nelson, Katherine Pretzler, Scott and Angela Pharr, Amena and Matt Owen, Mike and Deb Wilmot, Tom and Tiene Ruddy, Pat Heggy, Matthew and Jessica Turner, Shane Hipps, Matt Chandler, Donna Wynot, Melinda and Moises Ysagure, Monica and Dave Kirk, Phil and Debbie Waldrep, the Women of Joy team, Shanna Seyer, Jana Reiss, Melissa Leech, Esther and Bob Burroughs, Jinger Sellinger, Erin Bentley, Boyce and Shelly Ingram, Trevor Bron, Barbara Seibert, Angela and David Scheff, The Oas Family, Bill and Kris Zimmerer, The Grant Family, Shelly Miller, Cynthia Smith, Roxanne Nanney, Evan Rosa, Donna Bostick, Kathleen Brooks, Courtney DeFeo, Nicole Hutchinson, Michael Harrison, John and Lisa Carnes, Will Franz, Alicia Roark, Kathi Sturgeon, Thomas and Stacey Coffee, The Maher Family, our friends at The Chapel, Melissa Baldino and the team at *America's Test Kitchen*, Leith Anderson, Karen Malzahn and the NAE Staff. And to Jon Stewart, who always provided a good laugh late at night.

Abundant thanks to everyone who sent cards and texts and prayers and video birthday wishes—thank you, thank you, thank you!

Notes

.000 | Why We Live Joyless Lives

6 ***C. S. Lewis once described joy as "serious business":*** C. S. Lewis, *Letters to Malcolm: Chiefly on Prayer* (San Diego: Harvest, 1964), 92–93: "Joy is the serious business of heaven."

.001 | A Choice That Changed Everything

11 ***20 percent of mammograms miss finding dangerous masses:*** "Mammograms," National Cancer Institute Fact Sheet, National Cancer Institute at the National Institutes of Health, http://www.cancer.gov/cancertopics/factsheet/detection/mammograms.

18 ***I define joy as a spectrum of emotions, actions, and responses:*** To better understand the breadth of joy God wants to give us, check out *Fight Back With Joy* DVD Bible Study filmed with LifeWay. For a sample session or to order, visit www.margaretfeinberg.com.

20 ***"God saw that it was good":*** Genesis 1:4, 10, 12, 18, 21, 25 NIV.

20 ***"It was very good":*** Genesis 1:31 NIV.

20 ***the kind of creative high an artist experiences upon completion of a great work:*** Karl Löning and Erich Zenger, *To Begin with, God Created . . . : Biblical Theologies of Creation* (Collegeville, MN: Liturgical, 2000), 68.

20 ***"Then I was constantly at his side . . .":*** Proverbs 8:29–31 NIV.

21 ***his beloved Son, with whom he is "well pleased":*** Matthew 3:17.

21 ***a cheerful word:*** Proverbs 12:25.

21 ***a surprise birthday party:*** Job 3:7.

21 *a good day's work:* Ecclesiastes 3:13.

21 *an aged bottle of Merlot:* Judges 9:13.

21 *extra virgin olive oil:* Psalm 104:15.

21 *just out-of-the-oven artisan bread:* Psalm 104:15.

21 *sex:* Song of Songs 1:4.

21 *the birth of a child:* Psalm 127:3.

21 *a fiftieth wedding anniversary:* Proverbs 5:18.

21 *the dawn of harvest season:* Isaiah 9:3.

21 *. . . and more:* Psalm 104:15.

21 *his goodness extends to all humanity:* Matthew 5:45.

21 *promised a new dimension of life and joy:* The exact cause of this expanded capacity for joy is debated. Some attribute it to the removal of sin. Others suggest the quality or intensity of joy bumps up among those who believe. Whatever the cause, those who are redeemed should live palms up, ready to receive God's rich gifts expressed through creation and experienced through redemption, and keep in mind that even these most wondrous gifts are only foretastes of what we will experience when we live in heaven as we spend the rest of eternity with him.

22 *forgiveness:* Psalm 32:1–2.

22 *restoration:* Psalm 30:11.

22 *salvation:* Psalm 51:12.

22 *comfort:* Psalm 94:19.

22 *the law and decrees:* Psalm 119:111.

22 *God's presence:* Isaiah 12:6.

22 *homecoming:* Isaiah 35:10; 60:15.

22 *give ourselves wholly to Christ:* Luke 15:10.

22 *"I bring you good news of great joy . . .":* Luke 2:10.

22 *"These things I have spoken to you . . .":* John 15:1.

22 *"See, I will create new heavens . . .":* Isaiah 65:17–19 NIV.

23 ***this life is not the end of the story:*** I am indebted to Terence E. Fretheim's essay "God, Creation, and the Pursuit of Happiness" for the thoughts and biblical insights throughout this chapter. See also Strawn A. Brent, ed., *The Bible and the Pursuit of Happiness: What the Old and New Testaments Teach Us about the Good Life* (New York: Oxford University Press, 2012), 32–55.

.002 | The Living, Breathing Gift of Joy

30 ***a bizarre description of the size of a cow tongue:*** I double-dog dare you to Google the size of cow tongue.

31 ***his letter to Philemon is directed toward one member:*** William Morrice, *Joy in the New Testament* (Grand Rapids: Eerdmans, 1984), 126.

32 ***"Your love has given me great joy . . .":*** Philemon 1:7 NIV.

32 ***rabble-rousing, belligerence, and badmouthing:*** Acts 13:50, 16:19–21, 18:12; 2 Timothy 4:9–10, 14.

32 ***kindness, loyalty, and generosity:*** Acts 9:26–27; Philippians 2:25, 4:18; 2 Timothy 1:16.

33 **paraklesis,** *a Greek word meaning "encouragement" or "comfort":* Strong's #3874.

33 ***a spark of sincere gratitude:*** Philemon 4.

33 ***the Greek word*** **anapauo,** *which suggests calming someone:* adapted from *New International Dictionary of New Testament Theology,* s.v. "refreshed."

33 ***Paul uses this same word four times:*** 1 Corinthians 16:18; 2 Corinthians 7:13; Philemon 1:7, 20.

34 ***the Greek word used is*** **splanchna,** *meaning "bowels":* Strong's #4698.

34 ***Someone who reminded him that he was fiercely loved:*** Notes for this taken from "Finding Philemon" preached by Troy Champ at

Capital Church, Salt Lake City, Utah, on February 2, 2013. Thank you, Troy and Suzanne, for being Philemons to us.

35 **gave me glimpses into the holy:** One well-meaning but unhelpful comment we received from people was, "I'll do anything to help." This popular response is thrown around whenever someone faces adversity, but most of my friends going through a tough time have been heartbroken by this false promise. The needs in seasons of great adversity are immense, and most people are ill-prepared to do "anything" it takes. One friend admitted, "We've learned to ask my friends who say they'll do anything, 'What does anything look like to you?' If they don't quantify their anything, we'll be hurt and disappointed." Rather than making the false promise that you'll do anything, simply ask, "What can I do to help?" That way you can decide if it's something you can or cannot do.

.003 | Three Simple Words to Set You Free

44 **"thorn in the flesh":** 2 Corinthians 12:7 NIV.

44 **Malaria? A herniated disc? We don't know:** It's believed that the beatings Paul endured would have meant a lifetime of back, neck, and leg pain, and possibly severe bowleggedness. Hardship descriptions include 2 Corinthians 11:25–28; Acts 16:19–23; and 1 Corinthians 15:32.

45 **"I rejoiced greatly in the Lord . . .":** Philippians 4:10–13 NIV.

45 **"I have learned the secret of being content . . .":** Philippians 4:12 NIV.

45 **"I can do all this through him who gives me strength":** Philippians 4:13 NIV.

48 **Greek word autarkes . . . means "self-sufficient":** Philippians 4:12. See Strong's #842.

.004 | The Biggest Myth about Joy

59 **"Consider it pure joy . . .":** James 1:2-4 ESV.

60 **Within each container, God is at work:** 2 Corinthians 4:6–7.

69 *plucking hair was an expression of mourning:* Numbers 6:18; Ezra 9:3; Jeremiah 7:29.

.005 | When You're Tearing Your Hair Out

71 *"You are blessed when the tears flow freely . . .":* Luke 6:21 MSG. More literal translations like the New American Standard Bible render this verse, "Blessed are you who weep now, for you shall laugh," but the idea is the same. Grief is not the antithesis of joy but often the accompaniment.

71 *The Greek word for "blessed" is* makarios*:* Strong's #3107.

73 *I decided to return to my Jewish roots:* My last name is Feinberg. Please forgive the pun.

73 *"theology in action":* For more information about Hebrew mourning rites, see http://www.rabbidebra.com/support-files/ritesofdeath.pdf. I am indebted to the insights from this article for this chapter.

74 *a period of mourning known as* aninut, *or "deep grief":* This time is often brief because the dead are buried according to the command to not "let the body remain all night" (Deuteronomy 21:23).

75 *The practice of* keriah, *or "tearing," has deep biblical roots:* Genesis 37:34; 2 Samuel 1:11.

76 *mourners rip the fabric of their garments:* A ribbon is sometimes used instead of a garment. Neither the garment nor the ribbon is torn in half. Mourners leave a few threads attached, symbolizing that as long as the memory is alive, the connection between the deceased and bereaved is never severed. (Source: http://www.rabbidebra.com/support-files/ritesofdeath.pdf, used with permission.)

76 *"God has given . . .":* Job 1:21.

79 *"You are blessed when the tears flow freely . . .":* Luke 6:21 MSG.

80 *write a lament of mourning or find a garment:* I've found healing and clarity in writing laments based on the Psalms. Some of my

favorite songs to rewrite in the grief I experience include Psalm 13, Psalm 22, and Psalm 74.

.006 | How to Throw the Best Party Ever

86 *weeps at the crumbled mess:* Nehemiah 1:4.

86 *team up to restore the walls of God's city and the holiness of God's people:* Nehemiah 2:17–18.

87 *fifty-two days:* Nehemiah 4, 6:1–15.

87 *"Do not grieve, for the joy of the Lord is your strength":* Nehemiah 8:10 NIV. The call to celebrate doesn't contradict that grief is necessary; rather, it expresses the sentiment of the writer of Ecclesiastes that there is a time for weeping and for laughter. We need discernment and both are essential. The Scripture provides us pictures of holy grief and holy celebration—including feasting during a difficult time.

87 *the leviathan:* Psalm 104:26.

88 *exclamation point on the character of God:* Proverbs 8:30–31.

88 *the Year of Jubilee:* Jubilee is seven cycles of seven years. Scholars debate whether the final year is inclusive or exclusive. Some consider the forty-ninth year Jubilee while others consider the fiftieth year the year of Jubilee as to not break the ongoing seven-year cycles of Sabbath. See Leviticus 25:3–4, 8–11, 20–22.

88 *dinner party where we all worship Christ together:* John 2:1–12; Revelation 19:6–10.

91 *Leif made his famous black-eyed pea hummus:*
Leif's Black Bean Hummus Recipe
2 15 oz cans of black beans (drained)
2 cloves of garlic
1 tbsp of olive oil
2 tbsp of lemon juice
2 tsp of cumin
1 tbsp dried parsley or cilantro

Place in blender for two minutes. Serve with tortilla chips, pita bread, crackers, or fresh cut vegetables including celery, carrots, and cucumber.

91 *food created points of connection:* In light of all the eating in the Bible, sharing of food is a fun and sound practice. In John 21, Jesus even made breakfast for the disciples and dined with them after the resurrection in a sense to reveal his humanity to them.

.007 | The Side of Joy No One Talks About

102 *Why would the Lord use evil to bring about good?:* Habakkuk 1:12–17.

102 *"I'm not leaving until you show up and answer me!":* Habakkuk 2:1.

102 *Habakkuk never tells us how long God makes [him] wait:* Habakkuk 2:2–20.

103 *"Though the fig tree does not bud . . .":* Habakkuk 3:17–18 NIV.

108 *the apostle Paul's instruction to "rejoice always":* 1 Thessalonians 5:16 NIV.

.008 | One Prayer You Don't Pray But Should

110 *whoever captures the land can marry his daughter, Achsah:* Judges 1:1–10. A parallel account of Achsah is found in Joshua 15:16–19.

111 *"She got off her donkey":* Judges 1:14 NIV.

111 *"What do you want Me to do for you?":* Mark 10:51.

111 *"Rabboni, I want to regain my sight!":* Mark 10:51.

112 *Jacob receives more than he bargains for:* Genesis 32:26. *Israel* means "one who struggles with God." Jacob doesn't need to be asked, "What do you want?" before he answers the question with boldness.

112 *asks God for a son and soon gives birth to Samuel:* 1 Samuel 1:10–11.

112 *Solomon makes a valiant request:* 1 Kings 1:15–21.

113 *"Give me a blessing":* Judges 1:15 ESV

113 *". . . give me what I need to survive"*: Judges 1:14–15.
113 *still track the levels of morning dew in the region:* see www.weatherspark.com/history/32341/2014/Negev–Israel
113 *"the upper and lower springs"*: Judges 1:15.
114 *thirsted for Jesus' sweet presence and pined to experience his provision:* John 7:37–38. It's worth noting that in the Greek Septuagint (LXX) Achsah asks for a blessing in the form of a "ransom" (*lutron*) of water. This is the same New Testament word used to describe Christ as the "ransom for many."
114 *how much more will our heavenly Father meet ours?:* See also Luke 11:9–13.
121 *The rest of our trip was equally enchanting:* Some of our favorite places in Vermont include:
Snowflake Bentley Exhibit: http://snowflakebentley.com/museum2.htm
Ben & Jerry's Factory Tour: http://www.benjerry.com/about-us/factory-tours
Cold Hollow Cider Mill: http://www.coldhollow.com
Rock of Ages Quarry: http://www.rockofages.com/en/gift-shop-a-tourism
Hope Cemetery: http://www.friendsofhopecemetery.com
Knight's Spider Web Farm: http://www.spiderwebfarm.com
Cabot Creamery: http://www.cabotcheese.coop
Lake Champlain Chocolates: http://www.lakechamplainchocolates.com
World's Tallest Filing Cabinet: http://www.roadsideamerica.com/tip/8782
Penny Cluse Café: http://pennycluse.com
Burlington Farmers Market: http://www.burlingtonfarmersmarket.org
Barrows House: http://www.barrowshouse.com

122 *We missed the filming of the show:* Not to worry. The following year we had the thrill of sitting in the studio audience of Leif's favorite cooking show.

.009 | You've Got to Give This Away

126 *Leif was a rock, but I knew he needed a break:* Leif asked me to add that whenever you face difficult situations, knowing your motivation, your needs, and your response under stress is critical. We have used a tool called the Birkman Method in our marriage and ministry since 2008. Understanding our individual wiring during this storm helped us strategically get through these times. Check out this resource at www.birkman.com.

129 *"It's more blessed to give than to receive":* Acts 20:35.

130 *"Give, and it will be given to you . . .":* Luke 6:38 NIV.

.010 | When Nothing Means Everything

138 *I wanted to go to sleep and never wake up again:* One of my sweet friends, Kate, shared that she never understood why her mom, who had survived five rounds of battling cancer, reached a point where she said no to more chemo. To Kate, it appeared her mother had given up on fighting the disease. But after hearing the gruesome details of the chemicals' effects in my young body, she began to comprehend the tough questions that have to be asked when you're facing a terminal illness: quantity of life versus quality of life. As The Queen said, many patients refuse the drug because it's worse than the cancer.

140 *shouted out on Facebook and Twitter with #prayforzero:* Renovate Church in Morgantown, West Virginia, developed a #prayforzero campaign to support all those in their congregation facing health challenges. They even made T-shirts as a sign of support and reminder to pray.

141 *"My daughter has just died . . .":* Matthew 9:18 NLT.

144 *"What if I could finally be healed?"*: Matthew 9:21 NLT.

147 *"But if not, be it known to you, O king . . ."*: Daniel 3:17–18 NRSV.

149 *only piece of the promised land Abraham owns at his death is the burial plot:* Hebrews 11:8–10.

149 *Moses . . . dies without ever tasting the milk and honey of the promised land:* Hebrews 11:24–28.

149 *John the Baptist's . . . faithfulness is rewarded with decapitation:* Matthew 14:1–11.

149 *Jesus . . . is brutally murdered:* Luke 22:39–46.

154 *died clinging to the hope that God could do the impossible regardless of the outcome:* Hebrews 11:13–16.

.011 | Life Is Too Short Not to Do This

162 *"Lord, who is it?":* John 13:25 NIV.

162 *"It is the one to whom I will give this piece of bread":* John 13:26 NIV.

162 *into Judas's palm with the instruction: do it fast:* John 13:27.

162 *He keeps the disciples fed and manages caring for the poor:* Mark 14:50.

163 *gape in silence, unable to comprehend what has transpired:* John 13:22, 28.

163 *Peter . . . offers an unholy trinity of denials:* John 18:15–18, 25–27.

163 *Everyone else runs for the hills like their hair is on fire:* Mark 14:50.

165 *"Father, forgive them, for they know not what they do":* Luke 23:34 NKJV.

165 *Jesus seems to hug him extra tight:* John 21:15–19.

166 **Pain inflictors** *break the silence . . . with cruel or cold comments:* Some statements to avoid include: "You poor thing," "You're going to be fine," "You should hear what happened to me," or "Here's what I would do if I were you."

Connection

MARGARET FEINBERG is a popular Bible teacher and speaker at churches and leading conferences such as Catalyst, Thrive, and Extraordinary Women. Her books and Bible studies, including *The Organic God*, *The Sacred Echo*, *Scouting the Divine*, and *Wonderstruck,* have sold nearly a million copies and received critical acclaim and extensive national media coverage from CNN, *USA Today, Washington Post*, and more.

Christianity Today recently listed her among "50 Women" influencing church and culture. She currently lives with her husband, Leif, and their superpup, Hershey, in Colorado. You can reach her at: joy@margaretfeinberg.com.

FREE GIFTS JUST FOR YOU

Phone and Computer Backgrounds

Download this FREE screen art for your phone, tablet, or computer. Email joy@margaretfeinberg.com to receive your free downloads.

Because more than whimsy, joy is a weapon we use to fight life's battles.

This practical tool will help you fight back with joy beginning today!

IF YOU LOVED FIGHT BACK WITH JOY

Awaken to the Wonder Every Day

Do you ever feel like you're going through the motions of faith? In the *Wonderstruck* book and 7-Session DVD Bible Study, Margaret Feinberg invites you to:

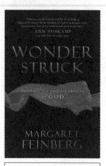

- Develop a renewed passion for God
- Identify what's holding you back in prayer
- Find extraordinary moments on ordinary days
- Discover peace in knowing you're wildly loved

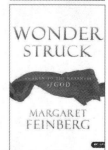

Visit MargaretFeinbergStore.com to order.